ALL ABOUT TREES

Created and designed by
the editorial staff of ORTHO Books

Editor
Barbara Ferguson

Designers
Craig Bergquist
Christine Dunham

Illustrators
Ron Hildebrand
Frank Hildebrand

Ortho Books

Publisher
Robert L. Iacopi

Editorial Director
Min S. Yee

Managing Editors
Anne Coolman
Michael D. Smith
Sally W. Smith

Production Director
Ernie S. Tasaki

Editors
Richard H. Bond
Alice E. Mace

System Consultant
Mark Zielinski

Asst. System Managers
Linda Bouchard
William F. Yusavage

Photographic Director
Alan Copeland

Photographers
Laurie A. Black
Richard A. Christman

Asst. Production Manager
Darcie S. Furlan

Associate Editor
Jill Fox

Production Editors
Deborah Cowder
Anne Pederson

Chief Copy Editor
Rebecca Pepper

Photo Editors
Kate O'Keeffe
Pam Peirce
Raymond F. Quinton

National Sales Manager
Charles H. Aydelotte

Sales Associate
Susan B. Boyle

Operations Assistant
Gail L. Davis

Administrative Assistant
Georgiann Wright

Address all inquiries to
Ortho Books
Chevron Chemical Company
Consumer Products Division
575 Market Street
San Francisco, CA 94105

Chevron Chemical Company
575 Market Street, San Francisco, CA 94105

Acknowledgments

Color Separations:
Color Tech Corp.
Redwood City, CA

Typography:
Turner & Brown, Inc.
Santa Rosa, CA

Authors

Franklin J. Chan,
Sacramento, CA
*Arborist,
City of Sacramento, California*

Francis Ching,
Arcadia, CA
*Director of the Los Angeles County
Botanical Garden & Arboretum*

William Collins,
Circleville, OH
*Staff Horticulturist,
American Garden-Cole Nursery,
Circleville, Ohio*

Contributing Editor
Lance Walheim

Consultants

Robert G. Askew,
Fargo, ND
*Extension Horticulturist,
North Dakota State University*

Maggie Baylis,
San Francisco, CA
Garden writer/illustrator

Russell B. Beatty,
Berkeley, CA
*Professor of Landscape Architecture
University of California, Berkeley*

Boething
Treeland Nursery Co.
Los Angeles and Santa Clara, CA

Bartow H. Bridges, Jr.
Virginia Beach, VA
*Self-employed landscape architect
and horticultural consultant*

L. C. Chadwick,
Columbus, OH
*Professor Emeritus,
Ohio State University*

John Copeland,
Norfolk, VA
Landscape Designer

Robert Cowden,
Walnut Creek, CA
Nurseryman and teacher

Morgan "Bill" Evans,
Malibu, CA
Landscape Architect

William Flemer III,
Princeton, NJ
*President, Princeton Nurseries.
Princeton, New Jersey*

John Ford,
Wooster, OH
*Curator, Secrest Arboretum,
Wooster, Ohio*

Fred C. Galle,
Pine Mountain, GA
*Director of Horticulture,
Callaway Gardens,
Pine Mountain, Georgia*

Richard W. Harris,
Davis, CA
*Professor of Landscape Horticulture,
University of California at Davis*

Francis H. Dean
Newport Beach, CA
Landscape Architect

Dr. James Foret,
Lafayette, LA
*Dean, College of Agriculture
University of Southwestern Louisiana*

William Gould,
College Park, MD
*Professor of Landscape
Architecture, University of Maryland*

Francis R. Gouin,
College Park, MD
*Associate Professor Ornamental
Horticulture, University of Maryland*

Richard Hildreth,
Salt Lake City, UT
Director, State Arboretum of Utah

Roger R. Huff,
Virginia Beach, VA
Arborist

John E. Kissida,
College Park, MD
*Professor of Landscape
Architecture, University of Maryland*

Clarence E. Lewis
East Lansing, MI
*Professor Emeritus,
Michigan State University*

Andrew Leiser,
Davis, CA
*Professor of Environmental
Horticulture, University of
California at Davis*

Raymond P. Korbobo,
New Brunswick, NJ
*Landscape Design,
Rutgers University*

Fred Lang,
South Laguna, CA
*Landscape Architect,
South Laguna, California*

Frank G. Mackaness,
Boring, OR
*Technical Advisor, J. Frank Schmidt
& Son Co., wholesale nursery,
Boring, Oregon*

Brian O. Mulligan,
Seattle, WA
*Director of University of
Washington Arboretum, Retired*

Robert L. Ticknor,
Aurora, OR
*Professor of Horticulture,
Oregon State University*

Frederick McGourty
Norfolk, CT
Brooklyn Botanic Garden,

Dr. Henry P. Orr,
Auburn, AL
*Professor of Ornamental
Horticulture, Auburn University*

Dr. Roland E. Roberts,
Lubbock, TX
*Extension Horticulturist,
Texas A&M University*

Warren Roberts,
Davis CA
*Superintendent of Cultivation,
Univerity Arboretum,
University of California at Davis*

Dr. Arvil Stark,
Salt Lake City, UT
*Garden Writer,
Salt Lake City Tribune*

Richard K. Sutton,
Lincoln, NB
*Assistant Professor of Horticulture,
University of Nebraska*

Dr. Carl E. Whitcomb,
Stillwater, OK
*Associate Professor of Horticulture,
Oklahoma State University*

Joseph A. Witt,
Seattle, WA
*Curator of Plant Collections,
University of Washington Arboretum*

ALL ABOUT TREES

CONTENTS

VIEWPOINTS
Page 5
Everyone places great value on trees in the landscape. People from all over the country give their personal view of trees and the effect trees have had on their lives.

HOW A TREE GROWS
Page 19
How to plant, water, feed, and prune a tree to encourage its proper growth. Descriptions and photographs of common tree pests and how to control them.

WHICH TREES
Page 41
Selecting the right tree means knowing how it will be used and how the climate will affect it. Tree lists and a climate zone map help you choose the right tree for your needs.

ENCYCLOPEDIA
Page 59
Complete descriptions of over three hundred popular landscape trees accompanied by color photographs and illustrations.

VIEWPOINTS

People have their own ways of looking at trees. To grownups, trees may be the key that unlocks childhood memories. To children, they represent adventure. To landscape architects, trees are a tool for creating different landscape effects.

Nearly everyone agrees that trees are important, even crucial—they provide shade from strong sunshine, barriers against wind, a play structure for active children, a canopied backrest for dreamy grownups, fruits, nuts, beauty, and so much more. But not everyone agrees about which trees will do well in specific areas, for specific purposes.

All About Trees is intended as a problem-solving guide for those who are concerned about which tree to plant.

This book is the product of answers to questions from hundreds of people. The responses came from every level of expertise—from people who couldn't tell the difference between an oak and a maple (but loved trees), to people who had devoted their lives to the study of arboriculture (and loved trees). More than anything else, this book contains the responses of people who have a deep commitment to trees. You'll find a lot of hard information here, as well—how to choose a tree that suits your needs, how to plant it, how to grow it, and how to maintain it. And to all the people who asked the questions, provided the answers, verified the answers, and then checked them again, we offer our thanks.

The following sources provided a wealth of information:

The University of Washington Arboretum
Seattle, WA

North Willamette Experiment Station
Oregon State University
Corvallis, OR

J. Frank Schmidt and Son, Co.
Boring, OR

Saratoga Horticultural Foundation
Saratoga, CA

University of California
Davis, CA

Los Angeles State and County Arboretum
Arcadia, CA

Secrest Arboretum
Ohio Agricultural Research and Development Center
Wooster, OH

American Garden-Cole
Circleville, OH

Princeton Nurseries
Princeton, NJ

Callaway Gardens
Pine Mountain, GA

Each grower listed has growing acreage of approximately 1,000 acres. The grower's judgment is particularly important, as he or she must gamble on which trees will be saleable three or four years after planting.

A backward glance

The questionnaire that we sent out to hundreds of people produced many hundreds of answers. One intense concern was voiced again and again: the concern that changing land use had cost us a heritage of trees. Many people volunteered memories of tree-climbing (and falling out of treehouses), of spring blossoms, of summer fruit, of autumn nuts, and of winter ice sculptures.

For example, one man who had a

We talked with people in Washington state, whose childhoods were spent among the giant maples and hemlocks along the Cowlitz River.

Left: The delicate flowers and foliage of the silk tree, *Albizia julibrissin,* complement each other and create a spectacular display in the summer. This display is most striking when the flowering tree is viewed from above.

A sycamore shades a house in Indiana.   Lombardy poplars still protect this deserted farmhouse from the wind in Utah.

wealth of rich memories remembered a childhood spent "living with the squirrels in the pecan tree," and "the giant maples, standing tall, shutting out the sky along the Cowlitz River, the hemlock that dipped its branches in the swirling eddy of the Snohomish." A Georgia man wrote, "Even now, I get excited every spring with the soft greens of the new foliage of the deciduous trees, and again each fall, when brilliant foliage colors the whole southeastern forest."

Another southerner recalled "a cluster of oaks, two of which had been bent to the ground at an early age and could be climbed and ridden like an elephant or horse. There was a treehouse built in three loblolly pines; the first floor of the house was 10 or 12 feet above the ground."

An easterner wrote, "I spent much of my childhood in trees, sometimes falling out of them. I vividly remember the sting of iodine being tenderly dabbed on my wounds (iodine can't be dabbed tenderly!)."

A Pennsylvanian told us, "I grew up in a steel mill town in western Pennsylvania. In spite of the filth of the town and the ugly, treeless downtown, many streets were lined with great sycamores. They made the crowded neighborhoods bearable and cooled the streets, front yards, and porches. They were dirty trees, shedding leaves, bark, and fuzzy 'monkey balls' in the fall, but they added so much to the quality of that dingy town."

A California woman offered a solution to the urban development that altered her home town. She wrote, "On our 99′ × 100′ lot we have created our own refuge. We welcome birds and squirrels; the skunks and raccoons investigate by night. Our goal has been to be able to look out any window and never see another structure. We have almost achieved that objective. It is a good feeling, the feeling of wilderness, even though we know that the neighbors we love are close by."

But our respondents shared more than just warm childhood memories of trees. They also expressed their sorrow that the big old trees—the kind that leave memories—have been cut down to make room for new developments such as highways, shopping centers, and housing tracts.

A northeasterner remembered, "There were still some woods in the suburbs when I grew up but bulldozers have cleared those woods for new houses. Few substantial trees have been replanted. It's a curious trait of some people—they'll clear a forest and plant dinky, trinketlike shrubs rather than shade trees. It's like collecting knick-knacks instead of designing a room for comfort."

Cherished trees have been diminished not only by the needs of an expanding population, but also by diseases and natural disasters. A Massachusetts woman told us, "I grew up in New England in an old Victorian home that had two circular driveways—one to the front and one to the back. Each circle had one majestic elm in its center. The Dutch elm disease slowly took both trees. We sprayed and pruned, but were unable to save either

one. To me those trees were part of the character of the house and the grounds. It has been 12 years since the elms came down, but I will never forget them." A transplanted Britisher recalled his school days in England during World War I. "The patriotic thing to do was to permit the felling of ornamental trees for use as pit props in the coal mine shafts. The loss of privacy resulted in the use of chestnut palings imported to England from America—hundreds of miles of pickets woven into wire strands, the wood derived from the trees killed by the chestnut blight."

A Texan wrote, "There were two old hackberry trees in front of the old farmhouse where I grew up and my parents still live. Many hours were spent under the shade of those trees on hot summer days, playing such games as boys play. A tornado destroyed the trees in 1969 and the house looks so bare."

Many people said that trees gave them a link to the past—a sense of regional history. A goodly number of respondents went so far as to state that trees are what determine the character of a place. According to one midwesterner, "Nebraska, except for the extreme eastern portion and along the stream courses, was a dry and windswept prairie. To the pioneers in Nebraska the planting of trees provided a sense of immediate security. They were a link with the immigrants' home in the eastern woodlands of Europe, they broke the force of the ceaseless wind, provided fuel for heating and cooking, shade from the hot summer sun, and visual relief from miles and miles of unenclosed space. The trees that survive here are symbols of the pioneer spirit that settled the state."

From southern California, a woman wrote, "The California oaks around our mountain cabin were multifunctional. They provided beauty, an 'outdoor living room' shaded from the unrelenting sun, the fun of a car-tire swing that hung from a high limb, and an appreciation that we were not the first to use this place. The rock formations under the oaks contained grinding basins where the Indians prepared their acorn meal many years before."

An easterner told of the town his grandparents had helped settle. "They planted seedlings from the surrounding woods. Sugar maples, red maples, Norway maples, and some oaks canopied the streets, forming cool, dark tunnels in summer. In the fall the chill of the frosty nights set the whole town ablaze with the celebration of color. The sidewalks became a great place to shuffle knee-deep through the leaves, which hid such pitfalls as chuckholes, ditches, and an occasional camouflaged skunk!"

In both a personal and a social sense, trees are our roots. They give us our sense of place. Again and again, our respondents voiced the desire to preserve the heritage of big, old trees for their children and grandchildren. A California man said, "My own kids don't have the same experience I had. There are only a few climbable trees in the neighborhood—too many pines and eucalyptus, which aren't good climbers. One great Valley oak used to support a long rope swing. The kids (including a few of us older ones) would play for hours swinging way out over the hillside. Now someone has bought the land and will soon build houses. People are willing to build playgrounds but don't seem to understand either the nature of Nature or the nature of play."

A Mississippi man reported, "My daughter and I were inspecting the trees we have planted in our yard and she said, 'I sure will be glad when they get big enough to climb.' That made me feel very sad, for she is eleven years old and the trees are only two years old. She will never climb among the branches of a 50-year-old mulberry in her backyard as I did—despite the fact that I knew my mother would tan my hide for getting mulberry stains on my clothes. Perhaps my grandchildren will be able to enjoy the pleasures of a tree swing or a good climb or a picnic in the shade of a big oak in Grandpa's backyard."

A man from South Carolina put the solution succinctly when he said, "The optimum balance between cutting and conservation must be reached if my kids are to have a rich life." Another man declared, "The only way we are going to succeed in preserving, conserving, and improving the trees we have is through

Trees provide standards by which to measure our human age (left: red oak)... our size (right: hard maple)... or our depth.

This backyard live oak in California adds to the mood of the wilderness setting.

teaching people about trees—or better yet, allowing them to learn."

Clearly, we need to review our priorities in many areas of environment and human habitat.

One southern California woman offered her experience: "My awareness of trees came very early and as an instantaneous revelation. One day, while enjoying the beauty of San Diego's Balboa Park, my parents pointed out to me the amazing fact that every tree, shrub, and flower in the park had been planted by man. I will never forget the impact of that first enlightenment: that it is possible for ordinary people to create enduring legacies of beauty through the planting of trees."

Another southern California woman wrote, "Our boulevards were lined with huge, old eucalyptus trees. They were very tall, never still, swaying gracefully in the gentle sea breeze. One by one they gave way to commercial development. Now there are none left. That section of our city is strangely bare, and we miss the pungent, medicinal fragrance of the eucalyptus on damp, foggy mornings. Yes, we miss those trees like old friends.

"On the positive side—we have the Wilderness Park in Redondo Beach. It was developed from a former Nike missile site and the entire park was designed to have the look of and to be a complete wilderness experience. The park is a little over eleven acres, located on one of the highest points of the city. Hundreds of trees were designed into the landscaping to identify the three separate camps. The 'pine camp' includes Arizona pine, Japanese black pine, Canary Island pine, and Aleppo pines. The 'gumwood camp' has several varieties of eucalyptus, and the 'sycamore camp' has many varieties of that beautiful tree. Natural wood and slumpstone bricks have been used in construction to keep the rustic look. There are two ponds with recirculating water to create natural-looking streams. The animals have already found this area, and add to the wilderness effect."

This seems to be the result of removing big, old landmark trees from the commercial and residential areas of our daily lives: We are compelled to create zoos where we can visit the trees that are no longer a part of our environment.

However, a Colorado woman had a very different experience with trees. She wrote of a scarred old pine called Old Monarch that dominated the landscape outside her grandparents' cabin in the mountains high above Denver. As a child she played in the aspen grove at Old Monarch's base and observed the eagles nesting in its top. Then one day a violent midsummer thunderstorm struck the tree with lightning, causing it to burst into flames, which moments later were quenched by a cloudburst. This woman told us, "After the storm we went to inspect the tree. The eagles' nest had been destroyed, but the eagles were very much alive. Old Monarch just had one more deep black scar to show for the latest onslaught. Grandma turned to me and said, 'See, honey, when your roots are firm and you grow to your full height, nothing can destroy you.' I was too young to understand the full meaning of those words but old enough to remember them."

The landscape architect's view

The landscape architect, from another perspective, is also concerned with these problems: how trees are affected by environmental and industrial pressures; the loss of trees through disease; the disappearance of trees from urban settings; changing land use; and the role of trees in reversing loss of community and sense of place.

Long ago, Garrett Eckbo wrote in *Landscape for Living*, "Trees, rather than buildings, are the best measure of a civilized landscape. A community in which many mature trees survive and more are planted regularly demonstrates a sense of time, history, and continuity on the land. It takes ten years or longer to produce a reasonably mature tree in most parts of the country. Few urban land users anticipate tenure longer than five years. This is not progress, growth, development, or vitality. It is insanity—a squirrel cage in which most of us chase madly round and round only to find the same old ugly city in the end.

"Trees as a primary landscape resource can do many things: establish a three-dimensional structural continuity throughout the community; establish pleasant connections and transitions between buildings, open spaces, streets, and fields; produce maximum greenery and climate control for minimum effort; provide the diffusion and filtering of light and heat which warm climates need; develop the sense of shelter and security."

More recently, Edward Holubowich wrote in the *American Public Works Association Reporter*, "A landscape designer is only one component of a complex team which affects ultimate density of trees and other physical environmental resources. City planner, architect, engineer, administrator, and politician must accept responsibility in evolution and

Trees dominate the landscape with their size, as shown in this park on Long Island.

Business districts

Business districts can be beautified with trees: They soften the lines of buildings, they give the street a sense of harmony, they pull together diverse elements, and their shade helps cool sidewalks.

Neighborhoods

Trees give neighborhoods their own character, enhancing good architecture and hiding bad. They also modify the climate, and create a pleasant place to live.

Junkyards

Trees can screen our junkyards, improving the view by hiding what is unattractive.

Industry

Trees absorb noise, filter the air, and limit the visual impact of industrial areas.

Skyline trees

Tall-growing trees create a skyscape and give a neighborhood character. They also add color to the skyline in the fall.

preservation of urban environments, for their decisions often profoundly affect the visual and physical quality of places where we live, work, and have fun.

"Once Man procures survival essentials, he starts to create pleasant surroundings that permit him to exploit his fullest potential. He beautifies himself and his immediate environment, then turns to the broader world around him. Nearly every North American urban area has examples of this phenomenon— stately homes with charming architectural detail, streets and boulevards lined with mature trees, neatly groomed parks and open spaces. We almost always 'show off' these areas to visitors.

"With the industrial revolution's advent, our society's attitudes toward environment in general have changed not only our economic emphasis, but have taken their toll in urban environment: paved and widened streets and highways and sidewalks claimed space; utility lines cluttered the landscape; the internal combustion engine in its myriad forms took away clean air. Yet all this symbolized progress.

"In haste to solve economic problems we've become willing to destroy some

This ginkgo, one of the best city trees, looks as indestructible as it is. See page 80.

natural environment. One of the most abused landscape elements has been our trees.

"An eminent city planner, Frederick Gutheim, says, 'Planting large shade trees must become a paramount objective of all who would improve cities' appearance. And it is the main hope for

any redemption of the lost character of American cities.'"

What Edward Holubowich calls "character," Ian Nairn calls "identity": "Townscape depends on two things: relationship and identity. It means making parts of the environment fit together— the supermarket, the gas stations, the car lots; identity is the recognition and enhancement of the specific needs and qualities that make one place different from another. And here, right at the start, a big warning: that no identity at all is better than a false one. The needs and qualities must be real, not artificially tickled up.

"In each distinct part of town you must be able to feel 'I am in it, I am near the edge of it, I am just outside it.' So that the town is a collection of distinct areas, not an amorphous gray mass."

Trees for your neighborhood

In order to create a neighborhood identity through trees, a community must select those trees that best suit and enhance it. How can you tell which trees to plant in a neighborhood? Here is the best advice we've heard: think of yourself as part-owner of the trees in your community. As a matter of fact, you are.

Each town and city should ask itself the following questions before planting any new trees:

- What distinguishes this town?
- Which trees have given this town its character?
- Which trees do best in this town's particular soils and climate?
- Which trees recall this town's history—its background?
- Which trees would make parking lots more attractive?
- Which trees could be used to screen out junkyards and other ugly spots?
- Which trees would enhance greenways throughout new subdivisions?
- Where can space be found for landmark trees—trees that are too big for small lots and narrow streets, or trees that reach far above the rooftops, high into the sky?
- Which trees would work for new expressways or freeways?

The towns and cities that have made the greatest progress in beautification (and, incidentally, the greatest increase in land values, as well) are those that have followed these prescriptions:

1. Plant trees to fit the existing conditions. Since downtown areas rarely have broad expanses of land or buildings setbacks, you'll have to make use of what there is—usually, only very narrow planting strips. Residential areas offer narrow planting strips in front of houses and apartment buildings, but new trees must accommodate overhead and underground utilities.

A grove of firs brings the forest into the city. See page 60.

2. Provide tree-planting space wherever possible, for every type of land use. Use trees:
— as screens, to separate residential areas from industrial areas
— to landscape industrial parks
— in building setbacks for street planting
— in greenway easements in subdivisions
— in wide planting strips between sidewalk and residential property rather than between curb and sidewalk
— in center parkway plantings on wide avenues.

3. Do all that can be done to preserve existing trees: develop good maintenance techniques; save valuable old trees from the developer's ax by making them "historical landmarks"; and plan developments and streets so that they bypass trees.

Tree preservation in Davis, California

Sometimes the issue is not planting new trees but preserving existing ones. Dr. Richard Harris, a teacher and researcher on the care of landscape trees at the University of California, Davis, tells how the city of Davis handled tree preservation.

"After a large oak tree was cut down to make way for a gas station near the downtown area, a way to preserve other trees from a similar fate was sought. Instead of trying to control removal of trees on private property by ordinance, the City of Davis chose an approach that would awaken public awareness. The city strongly encouraged, through approval of building permits, the rezoning and redevelopment of property.

"The city already had a strong street-tree ordinance that provided for trees in the commercial area. The street-tree committee surveyed all the mature trees of the city and designated fine specimens as either 'Landmark Trees' or 'Trees Worth Saving.' A tree was declared a landmark if it was: (1) an outstanding specimen of a desirable species; (2) one of the largest or oldest trees in town; (3) of historical interest; or (4) of distinctive form. The City Council memorialized these trees by ordinance and presented each of their owners with a resolution of commendation for having preserved them. Ninety-nine trees of 66 species were deemed of landmark stature.

"Probably of more influence on the appearance of the downtown area was the use of trees and large shrubs that were termed worth saving. As residential property was being developed for other uses, the city encouraged the developers to preserve as many trees as possible through the design and siting of buildings. Approval of building permits was an effective device. In the five years since this policy has been enacted, many handsome trees have been utilized to enhance the downtown landscape. The city took great care, when constructing parking lots in

Maples planted as street trees give a brilliant display of fall color.

the commercial area, to save as many large trees as feasible. The business district is a most pleasant place to visit because of the beauty and shade of mature trees."

About street trees

We talked to many arborists involved in street tree programs. Frank Chan, arborist for the city of Sacramento, California, speaks for all of them.

"Major emphasis on tree selection should be based on adaptation of the tree to the environment. Because of this, street tree recommendations will vary from location to location, depending on prevailing environmental conditions. In addition to adaptation, tree size and use should be foremost in our minds. The kind of street, whether it is residential, arterial, downtown, or mall street planting, makes a difference.

"A tree must fit the space where it is to grow. Overhead wires, underground utilities, traffic, and sign clearance must be considered. Damage to sidewalks, buildings, and other structures must be prevented or compensated for. Spacing between trees should provide for optimum growth as well as environmental and aesthetic enhancement.

"Trees should also be given adequate planting areas. Whenever possible, off-street planting in back of the sidewalk is desirable. Here, in the lawn or other landscaped area, adequate watering and aeration can be provided. Where there is much pavement and reflective surfaces of buildings, trees are limited by moisture deficiencies, poor aeration, and extreme

Street trees provide shade and air conditioning in the spring and summer, and a source of ready income when the leaves fall in autumn.

temperatures. Tree selection in these areas should be based on trees that can withstand abuse, and by size. Although the greater the environmental impact, with larger trees, the greater will be the maintenance potential and cost. Street tree selection should also be based on longevity, or expected life span. The longer the tree provides service and beauty, the more invaluable or economical the tree is.

"A large tree modifies the environment more than a small tree, making it possible to save on energy to cool or heat buildings. We need to preserve our large trees as long as is practical; however, we must also recognize when trees become liabilities. They should then be removed and replaced by the most promising or proven tree species of our time. We should use to our advantage trees that plant scientists have found to be resistant to pests and diseases. We should observe those trees that have performed well locally, and perpetuate them by asexual propagation.

"A basic requirement for a sound street tree program is the selection of adaptable trees to attain a diverse and well-balanced tree population. Street tree culture is a dynamic, evolutionary, and evolving process. It must be based on sound planning, management, and practices to assure that the community is getting the most for its tax dollars and that a healthy and aesthetically pleasing environment is attained. Because we have a wide variety of desirable trees, it makes sense to select more variety, in order to avoid high maintenance on a considerable portion of the plantings because of diseases or pests specific to any one group of trees.

"To maintain a balanced population, it is helpful to establish various percentage levels for trees planted in relation to the total tree population. This prevents overplanting any one kind of tree and avoids any enormous impact if a specific devastating disease or pest strikes, such as Dutch elm disease, chestnut blight, and, lesser known, ceratocystis canker in plane trees. Acceptable percentage levels for every tree species planted should be established by each community.

"The higher the tree population, the greater the need for variation. No tree should represent over 2 to 3 percent of the total population. Also, there is a need to use more tolerant species in the maximum percentage level. The lower the tree population, the greater the chance of using the most desirable species. Some species can be used at a rate as high as 4 percent to 5 percent of the total tree population without much chance of negative impact. The reason for this is you are using the most promising trees, and as the tree population grows, the percentage will be reduced if no further planting of that species takes place.

"Trees have a monetary value. However, no money value can be placed on them when, through the years, you have cared for and admired them. For this they have reciprocated by providing beauty and comfort. Indeed, a tree can be a long-time friend, and no money can replace this sentiment."

Who could place a cash value on the service these willows are performing?

The Lombardy poplar, often condemned as a "weed" tree, will thrive with little or no care. It is a good candidate for beautifying forgotten lots and "leftover" land. See page 97.

In defense of weed trees

And then there are those trees that seem to be no one's first choice. Weed trees, says Russell Beatty, Professor of Landscape Architecture at the University of California, Berkeley, are the unsung heroes of horticulture. "Have you ever poked through an overgrown backyard in an old, dilapidated section of town? Life may have gone out of the buildings, but an amazing thing has happened in the long-neglected garden. An abundant, almost luxuriant growth of trees, shrubs, and other plants thrives. At one time some sort of garden was carefully planted and tended. Neglected, and finally abandoned, a new type of garden took over. Many of the original plants died and fierce competition began. A strange ecological niche developed and the strongest and fittest plants survived. A system of plant succession developed very much like plant succession in a wild plant community. Delicate water-loving plants disappeared during droughts; vigorous drought-tolerant trees and shrubs grew undisturbed; low-growing shade-loving plants returned; birds brought in seeds from other gardens and neighborhoods, and the whole garden developed into a strange mixture of horticultural 'roughnecks.' They competed with each other,

lived on little nourishment, and adapted."

Who are some of these "dead end kids" of yesterday's gardens? The cast varies from region to region, but a few characters stand out clearly. There's the white poplar (*Populus alba*), which sends out its roots in its search for water, and creates new trees along the way. Its less invasive relative, Lombardy poplar (*Populus nigra* 'Italica') also appears from time to time. Other frequently found city trees are the silver maple (*Acer saccharinum*), common hackberry (*Celtis occidentalis*), and plum seedlings (*Prunus* species). In milder climates such as California's, you can find the blackwood acacia (*Acacia melanoxylon*) and a number of other imported exotics. For the most part, these weed trees are the outcasts of the plant world, scorned by horticulturalists and nurseries.

Too often, municipalities think of urban trees only in terms of street and park plantings. This attitude limits not only their choice of trees, but also the areas in which trees can be put to good use. Cities have visual and ecological planting needs that might be well served by the outcast weed trees. Such uses might include vacant lots, industrial areas, drainage channels, bits of leftover land in shopping areas, certain types of parking

lots, and perhaps children's play areas where little else can grow.

For example, the typical urban schoolyard has vast stretches of monotonous asphalt desert, is absolutely treeless, and is visually sterile. School districts characteristically are unwilling to integrate shade trees into the play environment. Most of the attempts that have been made have failed because the trees have not been maintained, or because of inadequate cultural conditions for the trees planted.

But instead of planting "desirable" trees that require sensitive treatment or vigilant upkeep, why not plant selected weed trees? Better yet, why not enlist the students? A landscape architect or horticulturist could be used to help make design decisions to determine the most effective placement of the trees. Then the students could take on the project as part of their studies. The "pride of ownership" that they would feel would almost certainly guarantee the success of their plantings. Perhaps they would decide to replace a number of large, underused asphalt areas with clumps or with masses of trees. Or perhaps they might choose to plant areas between activity courts with rows of individual trees placed in holes in the asphalt.

Street trees—a checklist

Choosing trees for a community is no simple task, but it helps if you know which factors to consider.

- How much space is there between sidewalk and curb? How good is the soil in terms of depth, drainage, fertility, moisture, and aeration? Can it be improved?
- Are there overhead lines or underground utilities or sewers to consider?
- Will trees interfere with street lighting or parking?
- What kind of street is it—residential, expressway, business? Is the street likely to stay the same size, or will it be widened?
- Is the tree the right shape and size for the site?
- Is the tree hardy enough for the area?
- Will the tree make a lot of work for maintenance personnel?
- Is the tree likely to get the water, pruning, feeding, and cleanup it may need?
- Will the tree tolerate pests and diseases?
- Does the tree do something special for the street, in terms of flowers, fruit, shade, or shape?

The off-street planting concept

Off-street planting solves many street problems. As Richard Harris of the University of California, Davis, puts it, "Public utilities, city street departments, and home owners have been faced with a street design that includes a planting strip which at best is usually much too narrow. This has resulted in more frequent pruning for size control; in many cases unsightly trees and street scenes due to severe pruning; and damaged curbs, gutters, and sidewalks which are hazardous and costly to repair.

"Trees planted behind the sidewalks, particularly if there are no overhead wires along the street, will require little or no pruning for size control of either the top or the roots. With the off-street planting of trees, roots will be less restricted and further removed from the possibility of damage from salt used for ice control on the streets.

"Off-street plantings that are to provide a variety of tree species and planting arrangements must be carefully planned and developed to provide a pleasing street landscape that is reasonable to maintain. The fairly recent planned-unit developments that are now provided for by most cities through their subdivision ordinances allow for the greatest flexibility of sidewalk, house, and tree placement."

Large trees, such as these black oaks, can raise sidewalks and break curbs when they are planted in planting strips. They cause fewer problems and are easier to care for if they are planted in the lawn and the planting strip is reserved for shrubs.

Tree shortages

Communities may find themselves in the frustrating position of deciding which trees they want to plant, and then discovering that those trees cannot be found in large quantity. This is because the greatest quantity of trees growing now are those that were planted in the greatest quantity over the last ten years. For a few years after their introduction, "new trees"—whether they are rediscovered old trees, trees that are new to an area, or brand-new introductions—are invariably in short supply.

The New Jersey Federation of Shade Tree Commissions (College of Agriculture, Rutgers University) has a solution for buying trees that are not currently available. The city places funds in escrow to cover a contract with a tree grower, who agrees to grow and deliver special trees in two to five years.

Private collections

Tree collectors collect trees for the same reason that people collect anything—because they love them. Some tree collectors begin quite innocently. They decide, for example, that they want to grow that exquisite blue-flowering tree they saw in Mexico last year, even though they live in upstate New York. The fact that both seeds and seedlings are nearly impossible to find only makes them more determined. They study the native habitat and reproduce it as closely as possible. They read books and ask questions (which are often unanswerable, since nobody's done it before). And that is the great contribution tree collectors make—they are constantly testing the range, tolerance, and adaptability of exotic trees.

Tree collecting is a natural byproduct of travel. Captain Cook's botanical expeditions brought specimens back to Kew Gardens; returning vacationers arrive home with seeds in their pockets as well as snapshots in their wallets. When you see something you've never seen before and must have, or when you have something you can't give up and need to take with you, that's when a bona fide collection begins.

Unusual flowers, curious fruit, and odd leaf structure, or bark texture, or branching pattern, or trunk shape can all be the basis of a collection. When is a tree defined as rare? Perhaps it is being grown well out of its natural range; or perhaps there are very few of them in the world. Trees, like animals, are constantly evolving; some species become extinct or near extinction. The role of the collector who obtains and grows such trees is that of the curator of a living museum. Collectors frequently make use of local arboretums and botanical gardens to get ideas or information, or to share their own experiences about growing trees. Arboretums have large collections of many kinds of trees, both common and rare. Some will sell or give away seeds or cuttings of their trees; all will answer questions. Universities and colleges often have botanical gardens with unusual specimens. If they don't have seeds to give or sell you, they should be able to get you in touch with a retailer or an organization that does.

Communities, as well as individuals, can benefit from the collecting spirit. Any arboretum, botanical garden, or university that will sell unusual seeds or cuttings to individuals will also sell them to cities and towns. While it might not be practical or desirable to populate an entire park with exotic trees requiring unusual habitats, a few well-placed rare trees—say, in front of a dull concrete civic building—can cause glassy-eyed passersby to stop, wind down, wake up, and appreciate the marvels of nature.

Both the tulip tree (top) and the ginkgo (bottom) have unusual leaves. In addition, the tulip tree is one of the few street trees with large and interesting flowers. See pages 86 (tulip tree) and 80 (ginkgo).

Selecting trees for a city

Selection of trees for your city may now be in the hands of some municipal authority. You may have a tree ordinance. But regardless of how your tree problems are being handled, it's important that local citizens be involved. The more attention and support a program receives from its citizens, the more effective the program will be. One way to encourage greater participation is to establish a "Tree Commission" through a tree ordinance. To get a copy of such an ordinance, write to the New Jersey Federation of Shade Tree Commissions, Rutgers University College of Agriculture, New Brunswick, New Jersey.

New trees for old cities

If you are selecting trees to compensate for adverse city situations, your choice is far more limited than when choosing trees to be planted in open spaces. As the demand for trees for special situations has increased, more and more growers have been selecting trees for special form and growth characteristics—such as narrow top, globe-shaped head, compact growth that fits beneath utility wires, better fall color, and no messy fruit or pods. These selected trees are then propagated vegetatively—that is, by grafting, budding, or stem cuttings rather than by seed. Such trees are called "cultivars," short for *culti*vated *var*ieties (a name within single quotes refers to a cultivar). Trees produced vegetatively have the same form and growth habits as the mother plant.

If the selected form is distinctly different, then a patent usually is applied for, or the grower's name for the tree will be trademarked. This special naming has been criticized by some on the grounds that the differences between the standard variety and the named variety were at times too slight to warrant singling out the tree.

Nevertheless, the naming of special trees has given us guidelines to predictable performance—ginkgos that don't produce fruit; ashes that are seedless. Norway maples and honey locusts, for example, now come in a variety of shapes and sizes undreamed of by the people who first planted our cities. The lists in the following chapter include a number of nursery-named cultivars.

The introduction of new cultivars has greatly widened the arena of trees to choose from. With the many selected forms available today, what was once one tree may now be a choice of eight different cultivars developed from the original. This proliferation makes generalizations about the size and form of a tree meaningless. Instead of asking, "How big is an oak?" you now must ask, "How big is this particular selected variety of oak?" Cultivars also change as attitudes toward certain trees change. Bad qualities can be weeded out. For example, the old honey locusts were often blacklisted because of their sharp thorns. Most of the new introductions, however, are thornless.

The new cultivars have risks that the old seed-grown trees did not have. Seedlings of the same species vary greatly in many ways, including in their resistance to pests and diseases. A few trees in a batch of seedlings might escape cleanly from a problem that plagues all the others, because they have a mixture of traits from both parents. This isn't true of selected trees grown from cuttings or grafts of one parent. They share their parents' weaknesses as well as strengths. Since a weakness to a certain disease could destroy all the trees of that cultivar in a community, don't limit tree plantings to only one kind (see page 12). Instead, plant a mixed variety of trees that are suitable for the area.

It is no small accomplishment to renew an old city with new trees. Although the rewards tend to be on the subtle side, a more public form of recognition can also be had. Cities that have done a good job in using trees for a more livable environment should contact the following organization for recognition:

Tree City USA
National Arbor Day Foundation
Arbor Lodge 100
Nebraska City, NE 68410

Keep looking

Lists of "approved trees" may be extremely helpful for a community that is looking for trees to plant. But many such lists have built-in shortcomings: The selections are made by a consensus of several tree experts covering wide areas. This means that excellent trees that are planted in some areas only infrequently may be excluded. Often, valuable, locally adapted trees fail to make the general lists.

Therefore, no city should "freeze" its approved list. Instead, it should consider all new introductions and new selections of old trees. The more trials you make, the more surprises in climate adaptation you find.

This *Malus* 'Red Jade' thrives despite its downtown location. For a list of other tolerant trees, see "Trees that stand city conditions" on page 54.

A planting of trees, such as these maples, can lower both heating costs in the winter and cooling costs in the summer.

Other merits of trees

Trees and energy. You can reduce your cooling bill in summer and your heating bill in winter just by planting the right deciduous trees at the west and south sides of your house. Electricity usage studies show that shaded houses use 2 kilowatt hours (kwh) per square foot, whereas unshaded houses use 3.3 kwh per square foot. In fact, walls shaded by trees are generally 15 degrees cooler than unshaded walls in California's hot interior valley.

Although the savings may vary (from 10 to 20 percent), the energy-saving value of the tree is recognized in every climate.

Houses that are shaded effectively have less need for expensive air conditioners. Air conditioners that have

already been installed will perform more efficiently and less expensively if the house is shaded.

William Flemer III, of Princeton Nurseries in New Jersey, points out that in the Plains States—states that tend to have high winter winds—the use of trees as shelter plantings or windbreaks has significantly reduced winter heating bills. In South Dakota, for example, the fuel consumption of identical experimental houses was 25 percent less in a house whose side was protected by a tall windbreak than in a house that was exposed.

In the more sheltered eastern states, adds Flemer, where fierce winter winds do not tend to blow, savings are less dramatic but equally apparent. The same house was compared in terms of its fuel consumption from before it had a windbreak to after one reached the height of

the house. A savings of 10 percent per winter was recorded. In light of the large population of the eastern states, this savings becomes even more significant.

Trees and shade. The value of trees isn't measured in terms of money alone—there's also the priceless benefit of human comfort. Have you ever stopped to rest under a shade tree on a hot, still day and felt a gentle, refreshing breeze? Shade trees are the original evaporative coolers. A column of warmer air goes up through the tree, causing a slight breeze at ground level by "feeding" this thermal column of ascending warm air. So when considering trees for your garden or community, don't neglect to take the cooling ability of trees into account, especially if summers in your area tend to be extremely hot.

HOW A TREE GROWS

The influence of growth and proper care on the performance of landscape trees is discussed in this chapter by Dr. Richard Harris, professor and researcher at the University of California at Davis.

Trees are so much a part of our life, both in their everyday presence and for the products they provide, that we seldom consider how they grow—from street trees to orchards, from managed forests to trees grown just for beauty. Their seeds are so small and the final results so big that the transition is hard to conceive.

To become large, a tree must have a way for branches to get longer, it must develop a structure strong enough to hold it upright against the elements. All this is accomplished through its plumbing system, which transports water and nutrients from the soil to the aboveground parts.

Some trees are deciduous, shedding their leaves each fall, while the leaves of evergreens persist longer, usually about three years. Evergreen trees drop their older leaves each year. In fact, evergreen trees usually drop leaves for a longer period than most deciduous trees, but the number of leaves that drop from day to day can be so few that this leaf fall is not always noticeable.

Shoot growth

At the tip of each shoot, in tissue no larger than a pin point, leaves, flowers, and the support and conductive elements have their beginnings. This region and that of stem elongation are within the top one to two inches of the stem. Tree growth in height takes place only in shoot tips or from buds that will develop into shoots.

Shoot growth of some trees lasts for only three to four weeks in spring; on others, it occurs in "flushes" during the growing season; on still others it occurs almost continuously when conditions are favorable. The growth of trees with a single flush is determined the year before by the number of shoot initials formed in each bud. On such trees, shoot responses to many cultural practices will not show up until the next year. Response to fertilization would be a good example of such a delayed action. Annual shoot growth is a good measure of tree vigor, and is easily noted on trees that have just one flush of growth each year.

In order for shoots to grow upright, plants have developed the ability to grow toward the sun (heliotropism), and away from the pull of gravity (geotropism). However, to hold ever-elongating shoots upright, trees and shrubs form woody cells and have the ability to increase their number. Growth in trunk caliper (width) is by cell division and expansion from a thin cylinder of cambium cells. Inner cells conduct water and nutrients, and support stem tissues called xylem (more commonly, wood). Outside the cambium, the phloem conducts organic substances from the leaves to other parts of the tree. This outer cylinder containing the phloem is the bark. See the illustration on the next page.

As with shoot elongation, the amount of cambium activity differs in different species and under different climatic conditions. Annual rings are evident in most woody plants because wood formed in the spring has larger cells than wood formed later in the year. Wet and dry years are clearly shown in the annual rain record of the xylem of many trees. The width of annual rings can be used as a measure of the vigor of a tree in individual years.

Trunk development

In most trees used for streets, patios, and landscapes, a strong, upright trunk is desired. Lateral branches encourage the trunk's growth in width, but unless they are shortened, the total height of the tree will be reduced. Horizontal laterals are slow growing. In contrast, upright shoots are more vigorous, and are likely to compete with the leader.

When an upright leader of a tree is bent from the vertical, the new xylem forms "reaction" wood, which counteracts the

A well-developed trunk and branch structure create a dramatic winter silhouette.

Left: The bright green new growth of the Norway spruce, *Picea abies*, contrasts sharply with the dark foliage that grew the previous year. New growth darkens during its first year on the tree.

The parts of a tree and their functions.

1. *Leaves* produce food for the tree, and release water and oxygen into the atmosphere.

2. *Choroplasts* are the chlorophyll bodies within cells in which photosynthesis takes place in order to manufacture carbohydrates (starches and sugars) for the tree. They give the leaf its green color.

3. *Stomata* are specialized "breathing" pores through which carbon dioxide enters and water and oxygen are released. They close when water is limited.

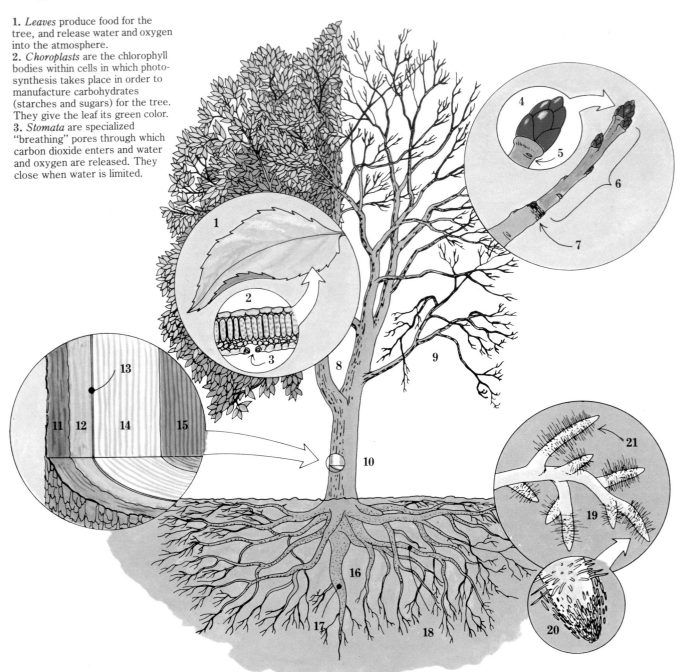

4. *Buds* occur at the ends of the shoots (terminal buds) and along the sides of the shoot (lateral buds). These buds contain the embryonic shoots, leaves, and flowers for the next growing season.

5. *Lateral buds* occur below the terminal bud at leaf axils. If the terminal bud is removed, a lateral bud or two will grow to take its place.

6. Each year's *new growth* is marked by bark of a slightly smoother texture and lighter color which will darken and get rougher with time.

7. *Bud scale scars* mark where previous years' terminal buds have been, and provide a means of measuring tree growth of many trees.

8. *Scaffold branches* are the large limbs that give the tree its basic shape and structure.

9. *Laterals* are secondary branches, mainly horizontal, that create the outline of the tree.

10. *The trunk* is the main support of the tree to better expose leaves to the sun.

11. *Bark* is the "skin," an external protective layer.

12. *Inner bark* (phloem) is part of the circulatory system, carrying organic compounds where needed.

13. *The cambium* is a layer only a single cell thick between the inner bark (phloem) and the sapwood (xylem). It produces the cells that allow both the phloem and xylem to grow.

14. *The sapwood* is produced by the cambium and carries water and nutrients up from the roots to the leaves.

15. *The heartwood* is essentially inactive sapwood. It gives the tree strength and rigidity and serves as a depository for stored food and wastes.

16. *The root system* can be quite extensive depending primarily on soil texture and depth.

17. Some trees may have an initial *taproot*, but as the tree matures, other more horizontally growing roots predominate.

18. The *lateral roots* develop at the base of the trunk and spread, forming an extensive network which serves to anchor the tree. They also provide storage for carbohydrates.

19. *Feeder roots* grow from the lateral roots and serve to transport water and nutrients absorbed by root hairs. They tend to be concentrated within the "dripline" (where the rain drips off the tree), but some may extend great distances.

20. *Root caps* produce a continuous supply of new cells that are sloughed off and serve to lubricate the advance of the growing root tip through the soil as it forages for water and nutrients.

21. *The root hairs* are microscopic appendages to the feeder roots; root hairs absorb water and nutrients the tree needs in order to live.

lean. The new xylem cells on the lower side grow longer than the ones on the upper side. This occurs not only in new growth at the shoot tip, but even on the trunk, where several layers of xylem have already formed. The forces developed by reaction wood can become great, bending trunks a foot in diameter back toward the vertical.

Trees that are subjected to wind form reaction wood to help keep them upright. However, reaction wood (when dry) warps, twists, and splits, and is weaker than straight-grained wood. Because of this, trees are planted close together in reforestation areas in order to minimize the wind effect and develop less reaction wood.

Each branch within a tree has a particular angle of growth, which it attempts to maintain by the formation of reaction wood. In most cases, more wood is formed on the lower than on the upper side of the branch. If a branch is forced from its angle of growth, whether up or down, reaction wood will attempt to return it to the original angle.

The formation of reaction wood does not always completely overcome changes of the trunk from the vertical, nor of branches from their normal angle of growth. That's why it's possible to train young trees or branches to desired shapes in the practice of bonsai and espalier. Bonsai is the technique of dwarfing a plant and training the branches into a desired pattern, while espalier is a method of training a shrub or tree into a flat pattern against a wall or fence.

If a branch or trunk is held for a year or two so that it can't, of its own accord, correct the angle at which it is growing, the new wood that's formed makes it difficult for the branch or trunk to return to its original, or neutral, position once the external force is removed.

Tree growth is influenced not only by wind and gravity, but also by light. Light has much to do with the direction of shoot growth and tree form. Almost everyone is familiar with shoot tips growing toward light, especially with houseplants. The tips of tree shoots react similarly. In addi-

tion, light can influence the growth of the trunk many feet below the shoot tip. Tests have shown that young trees tied to a single stake will tend to bend away from the stake. You can observe this easily by untying a young staked tree; invariably it will fall away from the side of the stake to which it was tied. Even if the tree were held upside down, it would still bend away from the stake. The new xylem cells formed on the shade side of the trunk are longer than those on the other side, and the trunk "tries" to grown away from the stake. This is why it is not a good idea to tie a young tree to a single stake. Light also plays a part in tree form when trees grow close to one another, particularly if the trees are different species or sizes. The branches growing toward a taller or more dominant tree will not grow as much as those on the more open side of the tree. In time, such a tree will appear to be growing away from the other tree. This may not be noticed by most people until the more dominant tree is removed for some reason. To develop their characteristic forms, trees should be given enough room.

Tree form

Trees come in all sizes and shapes. Their natural forms are largely determined by the growing tip of the terminal shoot. By observing how the shoot tip of a young tree influences the buds below it, you should be able to decide the form or shape of the mature tree even though you have never seen the plant before.

A shoot tip's influence on the buds below it in terms of whether the buds will grow or not is called *apical dominance*—dominance, or control, of the tip. The dominance of some tips is so strong that no buds will grow on the shoot below during the year that the shoot is growing. That the shoot tip is responsible is easily shown by cutting off the shoot tip. Soon one to several buds below the cut will grow. Apple, honey locust, and ash are examples.

Some species have weak apical dominance, so that a shoot grows from the axil of almost each new leaf soon after it is

formed. Liquidambar and tulip tree are notable examples.

Seemingly, trees with strong apical dominance would tend to be central-leader trees with one main trunk. But such is not the case; the next year, the terminal bud is not able to control the buds that were formed the year before. Of the ones that grow, several may grow higher than the original terminal growing point. While these laterals are growing, their terminals have strong dominance; but they, in turn, lose control the next season. As this keeps on for several years, branches are formed, which in turn are outgrown by new branches, thus forming a round-headed tree.

And yet trees with weak apical dominance—in which laterals form on the developing shoots—keep the laterals that do develop from outgrowing the terminal or the branches below. This control continues for a number of years, sometimes for the life of the tree. These are the typical central-leader trees, best represented by the conifers.

Not all species fall neatly into one category or the other, but the above are their general tendencies. As they mature, or become less vigorous, their growing points become more dominant, which makes for a more round-headed-tree form. Many conifers, for example, become round-headed as they mature.

Roots. The aboveground parts of trees depend upon roots for anchorage, water, mineral nutrients, and the production of certain organic materials. Tree seedlings may have either a tap or a fibrous root system. Most trees have fibrous root systems, although many young trees initially have a tap root system.

If the tip of a tap root is pinched, lateral roots develop a fibrous system above the pinch. This will lead to a much-branched root system that resembles fibrous roots.

If there are not internal inhibitions, however, roots will grow wherever soil conditions of aeration, moisture, temperature, nutrition, and soil tilth (that is, cultivation) are favorable.

Tree Form

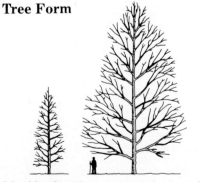

Liquidambar (Sweet gum) retains its conical shape throughout much of its long life as a result of apical control. It begins to spread very late in life.

Fraxinus (Ash) looses its strong apical control after the first year. Vigorous lateral shoots outgrow the terminal shoot, creating a round-headed tree after several years.

Pinus (Pine) is similar to *Liquidambar* and has strong apical control in its early years, which decreases as it becomes older. Some species become round headed at maturity.

How to buy a tree

Once you have decided to plant a tree, you can rightfully feel pleased with yourself: planting a tree is a good deed. You will be helping a tree establish itself in surroundings (sometimes hostile, compared to its pampered life in the nursery) that will be its home for many years. Even though nursery conditions may have been nearly ideal for rapid growth, a young nursery tree may not be well adapted for good performance in the landscape. Keep this in mind as you go through the checklist of things to look for in a tree at the nursery. Don't expect to find the perfect tree—you probably won't. But with a little looking, you can find a good tree; one that will live up to your expectations once it's been planted in the landscape.

Before actually buying a tree, read through this entire chapter. A good understanding of tree care will make the selection process much easier.

Not too big—not too small

Select a medium-sized tree. Many people think that the biggest of the bunch will grow the best, but this is not necessarily true. You want a tree of moderate size because the top and roots are more likely to be in better balance. Balance is more important than size. Look up as well as down.

Most field-grown, deciduous trees are undercut, dug, and handled with little or no soil on the roots; hence the term "bare root." Trees are dug in late fall and stored so that their roots are kept moist and their tips are dormant.

In the case of large, vigorous trees, a large proportion of their roots is cut and left in the field when the trees are dug. This low root-to-top ratio means that you must do more severe pruning in order to reduce the top to a size where the roots can supply it with sufficient water during the first warm days after the leaves begin to grow. If the tree is left unpruned, the end result may be a smaller, less vigorous tree.

Most field-grown evergreen trees are dug with soil around the roots. The soil ball is wrapped in burlap—thus this method of handling is called "ball and burlap" (B&B). The bigger the tree, the bigger the rootball. If different sizes of trees with similar size rootballs are dug, the ones with larger tops may have poorer vigor because of poor root-to-top ratio.

Container-grown trees offer greater uniformity, more ease of handling, and increased mechanization. There has been a surge of container-grown trees over the last 20 years. Nurseries must exercise skill and careful planning to ensure the vigor of container-grown trees. Of a group of containerized trees that are all

the same size, a medium-sized tree stands the best chance of satisfactory performance.

To sum up, then, whether you're buying a bare-root, balled-and-burlapped, or container-grown tree, avoid both the smallest and the largest of a group. For whatever reason, the smallest's less-than-average growth is likely to continue. And the vigor of the largest ones may be hampered by a low root-to-top ratio.

Root quality

The quality of a tree's roots at the time of planting cannot be overstressed; certain root defects can doom a tree to death or poor growth. A young tree's top is not necessarily a good indicator of the quality of its root system.

A well-formed root system is symmetrically branched, with the main roots growing down and out to provide trunk support. Container-grown and balled-and-burlapped plants should have fibrous roots that are sufficiently developed so the rootball will retain its shape and hold together when removed from the container, or when the ball is moved. The main roots should be free of kinks (sharp bends in the roots) and circles (roots that wrap around themselves or the outside of the container).

Kinked and circling roots, if not corrected, can cause such weakness that the tree cannot stand upright without support. Girdling is any injury to stems or roots that results in the restriction of the movement of water, nutrients, and food: Circling roots may girdle the trunk of the tree, causing it to grow poorly and possibly to die.

To check for kinked or circling roots, brush away the soil from the top of the rootball or stick your finger in the top two to three inches near the trunk. You can usually see or feel kinked or circling roots at the top of the rootball. Roots that look damaged, broken, or abraded are probably girdled.

The trunk—straight and tapered

Ideally, the tree you select should have a straight, tapered trunk that can stand by itself. It should bend evenly in the wind, like a fishing pole. Half the leaf area should be along the lower two-thirds of the trunk, with branches along its entire length. But trees pruned in this manner are rare. Commonly the branches are all located along the top half of the trunk and the tree is tightly tied to a stake. If this is the case, try to select a tree that can stand by itself when the stake is removed and be sure to protect the bare lower trunk from sunburn after the tree is planted. See "Planting," on page 25.

An unstaked tree is a better buy than a staked one. Read the section on staking before you buy (pages 28 and 29).

An easy way to check for adequate trunk development is to untie the tree

from its stake and bend the top to one side. It should bend evenly along the trunk and return to within 20 to 30 degrees of vertical. If it doesn't, look for a stronger tree. If you can't find one, you can buy the one you're looking at—but bear in mind that you must provide special care in order for your tree to develop properly in the landscape.

Before you select a tree, check to see if it has been headed. This is a method of pruning a weak leader back to a side branch or bud to encourage more compact growth. Headed trees in leaf will have several branches close together growing from below the cut; look for pruning scars on trees that are out of leaf. The drawback to trees that have been headed is that they may need corrective pruning if the new branches do not have enough space between them.

The bark should be free of injury from staking or improper handling.

Avoid buying sunburned trees. Sunburn may be common on newly planted trees that have been exposed to the afternoon sun, or that have trunks with few or no leaves. Split, flattened, or dull-colored bark are indicators. Sunburned trunks are extremely slow to heal and are subject to borer infestation. See page 38.

Foliage

If the tree is in leaf, its foliage is a good indicator of tree condition. Leaves should be dark green and evenly colored. Scorched edges or unusual yellowing are signs of problems.

Care after buying

It's just as important to take proper care of the tree after you've bought it as it is to choose and plant it properly. Keep it moist and cool (especially if it's a bare-root tree) so that buds won't grow before the tree is planted. You can keep it in cold storage, bundled with moist packing material around the roots. If necessary, you can delay planting a tree that's in cold storage two to four weeks beyond the usual time because the buds will be delayed in opening.

Bareroot plants can also be "heeled-in" for a short period near the planting site, preferably in shade to prevent moisture loss and to keep buds dormant. To heel-in a tree, cover the roots with moist sawdust or soil, working it in around the roots to avoid air pockets. If the plants must be heeled-in in the open, set them in a trench so that their tops lean toward the southwest.

Most containers are made of dark-colored materials. If plants in these dark containers are left exposed to the sun, soil temperatures near the side of the container can get high enough to kill the roots. It is important to protect containerized trees from the sun, as shown in the illustration on the page opposite.

Bareroot trees

For a better selection, buy bareroot trees as early as possible after the danger of a soil freeze has passed. Plan to plant within two days of purchase.

1. Look for several good-sized roots going in different directions at various levels from the main root.

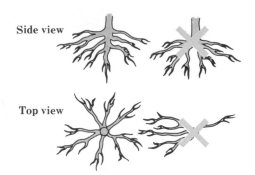

Side view

Top view

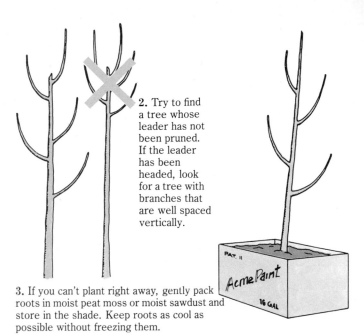

2. Try to find a tree whose leader has not been pruned. If the leader has been headed, look for a tree with branches that are well spaced vertically.

3. If you can't plant right away, gently pack roots in moist peat moss or moist sawdust and store in the shade. Keep roots as cool as possible without freezing them.

Ball and burlap trees

Balled and burlapped trees can be bought and planted at any time of year, though spring is best. Choose medium-sized trees; they usually have a better root system in proportion to the top.

1. Untie the top of the burlap and look carefully at the rootball. You want a firm, solid ball of soil. Don't choose one that's cracked or broken, like the one on the left. The one on the right is a better choice.

2. Look for circling roots. If they circle the trunk at the soil surface, select another tree.

3. Until planting, keep your tree in the shade in an upright position. Keep the rootball moist by watering it slowly from the top. Also, wet the foliage occasionally.

Container trees

Trees in containers may be planted at any time of the year where the ground does not freeze. Buy medium-sized trees rather than the largest for a better root-to-top ratio.

1. Look for circling roots at the soil surface; these may girdle the trunk and provide inadequate support.

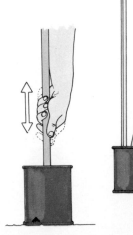

2. Lift the tree slowly by grasping it at the base. If the tree moves up before the can and soil do, the roots are not well developed.

3. If, when untied from the stake, the tree bends as shown, it has a weak trunk. Try to find another tree which can stand upright and has lower lateral branches.

4. If the tree will not be planted right away, keep the soil moist and wet the foliage occasionally. Shade the containers; you can use a board or cover them with peat moss or soil.

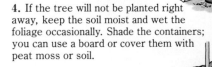

Preparing the site

A planting hole is really a transition zone in which the roots of a tree adjust from the planting mix of the nursery to the soil in your garden.

How large that transition zone needs to be depends upon the condition of your soil. To determine what your soil needs before you plant, explore a little—use a shovel, your fingers, or even a soil auger. Take note of these considerations:

■ Soil texture—the size of soil particles. Is your soil sandy, on the clay side, or a mixture of sizes (a loam)? See the illustration below.

■ Soil structure—the arrangement of particles. Is your soil of good tilth, compacted, or somewhere in between?

■ Soil depth—Is your soil deep enough so that a tree can anchor itself in it? Is it deep enough to drain well without restricting root growth and function?

Texture and structure

Most soils will provide a suitable rooting medium—one that holds moisture while allowing proper aeration—with little or no amending. In general, soils are a mixture of soil particle sizes of acceptable structure—in short, a loam soil. Such soils crumble easily when you dump a shovelful beside the planting hole, or manipulate the soil between your fingers. Just crumble it and use as is for backfilling.

Soils that are extremely sandy or clayey can be improved by adding organic matter (peat, compost, nutrified bark, or well-decomposed sawdust) to the backfill at a rate of 2 parts soil to 1 part organic matter. Sandy soils usually drain well and have good aeration, but they do not retain much water. To some degree, organic matter will increase the moisture-holding capacity of sandy soils.

At the other extreme, clay soils hold a lot of water but may drain poorly and have inadequate aeration. Organic matter will help improve drainage and aeration of clay soils by separating some of the parti-

Raised beds or berms

Redwood lumber

Berms

Add depth and improve drainage in shallow soil with a raised bed or berm (mound). Raised areas add to landscape interst, but may be difficult to irrigate.

Containers

Many kinds of trees grow well in containers. Containers are available in both wood and lightweight concrete.

cles to provide paths for water and air.

There's an easy way to find out what kind of soil you have. Pick up a handful of soil and squeeze. A ball of clay will remain in a tight, ridged lump. Loam will hold its shape, but will crumble if you poke it. Sandy soil will begin to fall apart as you open your hand.

To find out how well your soil drains, dig a hole and fill it with water. Let it drain, then refill. After the second filling, the water should drain about ¼ inch per hour. If it drains much faster, the soil is sandy and well drained. If it drains much slower, it is clay soil, compacted soil, or has a compacted layer below the surface.

Compaction

Soil around new homes, former paths or drives, or old farmland may be severely compacted. If your soil is still at or near its original grade, only the top 6 to 10 inches will be compacted. If fill soil has been brought in, the compacted zone will be that much deeper. In this case, make your planting hole large enough in diameter and deep enough to reach the soil below through the compacted soil. For backfill, use surface soil or soil from below the compacted layer, mixed with a little organic matter.

Shallow soils

Shallow soils may restrict growth and prevent the tree from anchoring fully. Such soil may be underlain with rock or hardpan—a layer of fine clay particles that have accumulated some distance below the soil surface to form sedimentary rock. In shallow soils, water may

Soil texture

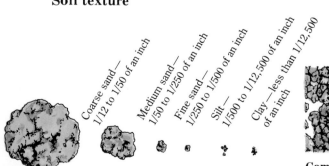

Coarse sand— 1/12 to 1/50 of an inch

Medium sand— 1/50 to 1/250 of an inch

Fine sand— 1/250 to 1/500 of an inch

Silt— 1/500 to 1/12,500 of an inch

Clay—less than 1/12,500 of an inch

Sand, silt, and clay are designations based on the size of mineral particles found in soil. The texture of soil is determined by the proportions of these various-sized particles.

Soil structure

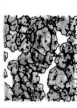

Compacted soil: The particles are packed with little space for air or water.

Crumbly soil: Organic matter aggregates particles into porous crumbs.

Saturated soil: If water doesn't drain through the soil, the plants may drown.

Moist soil: There is a film of water between soil particles with air in the larger pores.

collect on the impervious layer, where it may drown the plants.

If you have shallow soil, you have two alternatives: You can go either over it or through it.

To go over shallow soil, you can build raised beds or mounds and plant small trees. The mounds provide depth for root development, as well as better drainage. But don't plant trees that grow quite large and tall; these shallow soils will not support their root system. Raised beds have the advantage of making the tree the focal point in the landscape. Unless your garden soil is quite unacceptable, you can use it in the raised planter. Very sandy or clayey soil can be amended with organic matter. Loosen the original soil surface before filling the raised bed.

If the soil is completely unworkable, and some soils are, large containers may be the answer. A container lets you select a lightweight, well-drained soil.

To go under shallow soil, break through the hardpan layer with a pick, post-hole digger, or well-auger. Use only surface soil (or surface soil mixed with organic matter) for backfill. Allow it to settle, and plant as usual.

When you can't go through the impervious layer, be sure there is sufficient soil depth to anchor a tree and use a tile drain to remove excess water (see illustration).

Planting

Although orientation is not necessarily critical to the survival of a tree, it should be considered before you set a tree in its hole. Sunburn can be avoided if the tree is oriented properly. Place the scion (the bud or graft) of grafted trees toward the afternoon sun to reduce the possibility of sunburn just above the bud union. Low foliage may shade this area. If the trunk is exposed, you can paint it with white latex paint or wrap it with a commercial tree wrap.

Root pruning

Before planting, cut back any injured, diseased, twisted, or dead roots to healthy tissue. When planting container-grown trees, make sure that the bottom of the hole is firm and level. A slight rise in the center makes it easier to spread the roots of bare-root trees. Spread the roots in the bottom of the hole to provide good anchorage and to prevent circling.

For container-grown trees, cut and remove some of the roots that are matted at the bottom or circling around the outside of the rootball. In freeing the roots at the edge of the rootball, also break away some of the soil to provide better contact between the rootball and the fill soil. Removing one-fourth to one-half of the roots in the outer inch of the rootball of rootbound plants should not set back any but the most sensitive plants. If anything, most plants will be stimulated.

Drainage

When shallow soil is underlaid by a layer of impervious soil or hardpan, excess water cannot drain away. Here are some solutions.

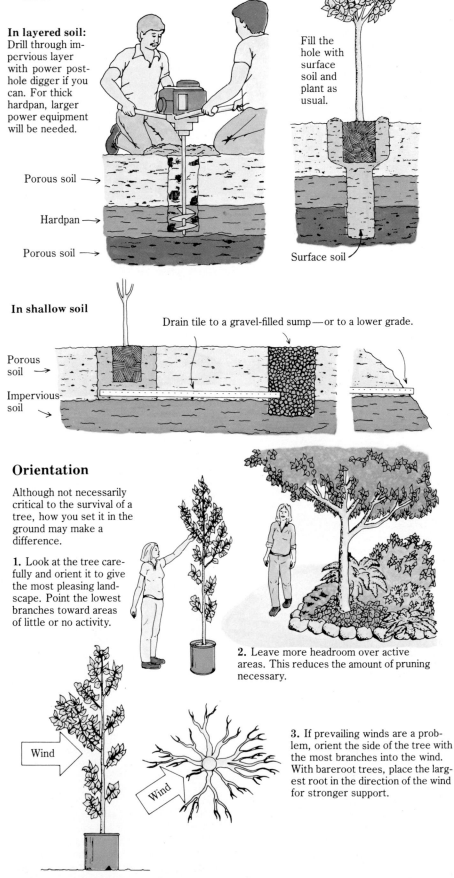

In layered soil: Drill through impervious layer with power posthole digger if you can. For thick hardpan, larger power equipment will be needed.

Porous soil →

Hardpan →

Porous soil →

Fill the hole with surface soil and plant as usual.

Surface soil

In shallow soil

Drain tile to a gravel-filled sump—or to a lower grade.

Porous soil →

Impervious soil →

Orientation

Although not necessarily critical to the survival of a tree, how you set it in the ground may make a difference.

1. Look at the tree carefully and orient it to give the most pleasing landscape. Point the lowest branches toward areas of little or no activity.

2. Leave more headroom over active areas. This reduces the amount of pruning necessary.

Wind

Wind

3. If prevailing winds are a problem, orient the side of the tree with the most branches into the wind. With bareroot trees, place the largest root in the direction of the wind for stronger support.

Pruning the foliage of new trees

1. Part of the top growth of a newly planted tree should be pruned out so that the roots and top are in better proportion.

2. Use a thinning-out type of pruning so as not to modify the natural form of the tree.

Top pruning

Even if no roots are lost during planting, the top of the tree may have such a large leaf area that frequent watering is needed to prevent wilting. You don't have to reduce the actual size of the top. You can remove considerable leaf area by thinning out branches that are close together, crossing one another, or broken, without affecting the plant's overall size. Removing a quarter of the leaf area from most trees will result in trees with little visual change in the plant.

Bare-root trees will probably need more pruning than container or balled-and-burlapped trees because they are dug up with fewer roots.

Some pruning may have been done at the nursery. If so, little more need be done. Check for pruning scars, or ask the nursery.

Placing the rootball

With balled-and-burlapped trees, fold back the burlap at least 2 inches below the soil level. Leaving it exposed creates a wicklike action that will dry out the soil faster than is normal. Carefully slice the burlap on the sides and bottom of the rootball to allow for easy root penetration.

Burlap generally rots away within a year; however, some burlap may be treated with a preservative for nursery keeping. If so, you'll need to remove the burlap before you plant. Ask at the nursery whether the burlap has been treated. If it has, gently rock the rootball to one side, pushing the burlap as far under it as possible. Then rock it back, and the burlap should be free. With smaller rootballs, it may be easier to just lift the plant away from the burlap carefully.

Backfill the hole with the original soil, unless that soil is undesirable. Add organic matter to heavy, extremely light, or compacted soils. See "Texture and structure" (page 24) for instruction on mixing backfill.

Don't place fertilizer in the planting hole or mix it with the backfill soil. This can injure the plant. Trees should be fertilized when new growth begins.

If staking is necessary, place the stakes after the tree has been planted. See pages 28 and 29.

Set the roots or rootball on a firm base, with the center slightly higher than the edge of the hole. This will help in spreading the roots and, to a certain extent, in draining water away from the base of the roots. Work the soil in around the roots so they are not compressed into a tight mass, but are spreading and supported by soil underneath. After filling in 3 to 4 inches of soil, water the roots and allow the soil to settle in by gently rocking the tree back and forth. The original ground level of the plant when in the nursery, or of the rootball, should be 1 or 2 inches above the finished ground level for clay or loam soils, and about even with the surrounding soil if that soil is extremely sandy. You can plant bare-root trees 1 to 2 inches deeper in sandy soil. If the trunk shows a dark-to-light color change below the bud union, this indicates the original soil level in the nursery.

Basins

Make the watering basin for trees at least 30 inches in diameter. Twice the size of the rootball is a good rule of thumb. A ridge 4 or 5 inches high (made of soil dug from the planting hole) makes it possible to wet the soil thoroughly.

Fill the basin with water to further settle the soil and to provide roots with water. This will improve the contact between the fill soil and the roots.

For several weeks after planting, the rootball will need more frequent watering than the surrounding soil, which has few

roots. To make certain that the ball receives adequate water, build a dike inside the first basin. It should be slightly smaller than the rootball itself. The inner circle will concentrate the water where it is needed. Water the inner circle thoroughly every 1 to 3 days for the first few weeks to ensure that the tree has adequate moisture. How often you'll need to water will depend on how many leaves the tree has, and on the weather. Check the moisture in the rootball by digging down a couple of inches to see if the soil is damp. After the roots penetrate the transition zone—4 to 6 weeks after planting—remove the inner dike. In the meantime, the outer zone will need less water (the amount varies with your soil type), but do keep it moist.

In areas of high rainfall, temporarily knock down the dikes to keep water from accumulating at the base of the tree. If you don't, crown rot can result, which may kill the tree.

If the tree settles so that the original soil line is below the soil surface, you can raise a bare-root tree slightly higher than you want it, then let it settle back into the soil. This gives its roots better contact with the soil. With container or balled-and-burlapped trees, use a shovel under the rootball to raise the plant. These operations should be done soon after planting, when the soil is saturated.

Raise the soil level as little as possible—the more the plant is raised, the closer the roots are drawn together. This weakens anchorage and reduces the volume of soil that's in contact with the roots.

After the soil has drained, you can create the final contour of the basin—with the base of the plant slightly higher than the bottom of the basin. Then water won't collect around the trunk. Unless some soil has washed away from the top of the rootball, don't construct the contour of the final basin by adding soil to the top—especially if the backfill soil is heavier than that of the rootball, which would make the rootball difficult or impossible to wet.

Competition from turf. When trees are planted in a lawn area, keep the turf well away from the trunk of the tree during the first two or three years. The growth of young trees can be retarded by grass growing close to their trunks, even if additional water and fertilizer are applied. Keeping a 30-inch-diameter area of bare soil around the tree will also keep young trees from being damaged by lawn mowers. Mechanical damage to the trunks of young trees can severely dwarf them.

Use herbicides in tree basins with caution. They can injure the bark of young trees. Follow the manufacturer's directions closely.

See page 31 for mulching instructions.

Ball and burlap planting

1. Carefully set the wrapped rootball into the hole. The soil line of the tree should be slightly higher than the surrounding soil. Remove any ties around the rootball.

2. Fill the hole with backfill soil, firming it down as you go.

3. Cut the burlap away from the trunk and be sure all edges are buried well below the soil surface to prevent wick action from drying out the rootball.

Container planting

1. Gently knock the tree out of the container and remove circling or matted roots.

2. Set the tree carefully into the hole. Be sure the soil line of the tree is slightly higher than the surrounding soil.

3. Add and firm backfill soil gradually to assure good root contact.

Bareroot planting

Soil line
Broken
Twisted
Discolored

1. Before planting, trim off any broken, twisted, or discolored tips. Determine the location of the original soil line by the change of color on the trunk.

2. Set the tree in the hole so the soil line is above the surrounding soil. Spread roots evenly. Keep them radiating out from the root crown.

3. Work backfill soil between and around the roots. Firm the soil gently as you fill the hole, making certain roots and soil are in contact.

4. Eliminate air pockets, settle soil, and bring soil into firm contact with the roots by running water slowly over the root area.

Check planting depth

After watering to settle the soil, check to be certain the original soil line is not buried. If it's too low:

Bareroot: Grasp the trunk near the soil and lift an inch or two higher than the proper level and then let the tree settle back.

Ball and burlap or containers: Carefully place a shovel beneath the rootball and pry up while lifting on the trunk. Raise it an inch or two above the proper level and let it settle back.

Water again, if necessary, to resettle the soil.

Basins

1. Build a shallow basin so water soaks down into the rootball with a minimum of run-off.

2. With all of the tree's roots still in the rootball, the soil in the rootball will dry faster than the surrounding soil. To improve rooting conditions and save water, build a double basin system. Use the rootball-width basin for primary watering until some roots have grown into the surrounding soil.

When good trees go bad

If the soil is ideal, the whole planting process requires common sense. After all, many a tree has been grown without the attention outlined here. But things do go wrong. Before blaming the nursery if your tree doesn't grow, check the following points.

■ Has the tree settled? Check the planting depth. Many trees die from crown rot that occurs because the soil settled after you planted the tree.

■ Has the tree dried out? Until their roots can spread into the surrounding soil, container or balled-and-burlapped trees should be watered more often than if they were still in their respective packaging. Remember, a transpiring tree uses water faster from its rootball than moisture evaporates from open ground. Don't let the fact that the surrounding soil may be wet mislead you—the rootball of a newly planted tree may have dried out despite the moisture up above.

Be your own Johnny Appleseed

If you have a large bare area to plant and are in no rush for quick effect, seeds may be your easiest and cheapest solution. Even in areas with only 10 inches of annual rainfall and a long rainless growing season, trees and shrubs will become established if given a little additional care. However, trees grow faster when there's more rain and weeds are not a problem.

If you want to give seeds a try, keep these things in mind. Select species that you know will do well in your area. Check with your local nursery or horticulturist to find out if any special treatment is needed to overcome possible seed dormancy. If your soil does not freeze during winter, plant the seeds in fall when rains have wet the soil. Otherwise, wait until the soil thaws in the spring. Dig a small hole about 4 inches deep, put in about ¼ teaspoon of a nitrogen fertilizer, cover it with 3 inches of soil, place the seeds in the hole, and cover them with fine soil about three times their diameter. Three large seeds are usually enough, but add more if the seeds are fine.

If more than one plant grows in a hole, pinch back all but the most vigorous one to give it the best chance to grow well. Leave the others until you are sure the selected one is established. If deer or rabbits are a problem, surround each seedling hole with a 1-foot-diameter, 3-foot-high cylinder of woven wire fencing held in place with two stakes.

Given good soil, 15 inches of winter rain, and no summer irrigation, several species in mild climates grew more than 6 feet in two growing seasons.

The importance of seed source location

Seedling trees may vary greatly in certain characteristics, particularly if the seeds come from different climatic areas. In fact, seed source may be the main reason for the common observation that some plants grow poorly when propagated and raised in a climate different from the one in which they are to be planted. For example, the natural range of the flowering dogwood (Cornus florida) extends from the northern parts of the United States to Central America. Trees grown from seeds from the southern range will not be as hardy as trees from the northern range. Also be sure not to plant eastern redbud (Cercis canadensis) outside of its range.

Here are some sources of tree seeds:

Carter's Seeds
P. O. Box 4006
Sylmar, CA 91342

Clyde Robin Seed Co., Inc.
P. O. Box 2855
Castro Valley, CA 94546

Native Plants Inc.
9180 South Wasatch Blvd.
Sandy, UT 84092

Stieghorst Seed Company
2070 Foothills Road
Golden, CO 80401

Plants of the Southwest
1570 Pacheco Street
Santa Fe, NM 87501

Lawyers Nurseries
Route 2, Box 95
Plains, MT 59859

F. W. Schumacher
36 Springhill Road
Sandwich, MA 02563

A World Seed Service
J. L. Hudson, Seedsman
P. O. Box 1085
Redwood City, CA 94064

Abundant Life Seed Foundation
P. O. Box 374
Gardiner, WA 98334

Southern Seed Company
P. O. Box 287
Baldwin, GA 30510

To learn all about growing trees from seed, use the excellent *Seeds of Woody Plants in the United States*. It's the standard reference book on the subject and available for $24.00. Ask for stock #001–000–029–02–9. Write to:

Superintendent of Documents,
U.S. Government Printing Office
Washington, DC 20402

Staking

A young tree that is exposed to wind and weather concentrates its energy on growing strong enough to remain upright. It develops a sturdy trunk that is tapered to bend without breaking, and a strong root system to hold this trunk in place. Unfortunately, some common practices prevent the young tree from growing as strong as it should. Nurseries try for a maximum use of space by placing trees too close together. Thus, the side branches, which could nourish the trunk and strengthen the tree, are shaded out or trimmed off. Then the tree is staked. These practices encourage height growth at the expense of trunk development. By the time you get the tree, it often can't stand without a stake. Ideally, look for a sturdy tree with some side branches that will strengthen the trunk. If none is available in the species of tree you want, you can stake it—but only until it is sufficiently established to stand on its own.

Sometimes thinning will be sufficient to reduce the weight and wind-resistance of the top. Sometimes tilting the rootball slightly will be enough to help the tree stand independently. Try these methods before getting out the staking materials—you may save yourself a lot of time and have a stronger tree, too.

Mechanical damage can have a severe dwarfing effect; even a sturdy young tree needs protective stakes to prevent damage from lawn mowers and other garden activities. Therefore, place three stakes, just tall enough to be seen easily, at the outer edge of the rootball and at least 6 inches from the trunk.

The trunks of many trees will hold their tops upright as long as the roots are firmly anchored. Anchor stakes can be used to hold the roots where they are planted until those roots become established enough to hold the tree.

You can use the same anchor stakes to protect the trunk and to hold the roots. To safeguard the trunk, wind loop or figure-eight ties between the stakes and the trunk. These will hold the roots and still allow the top to flex in the wind.

Support staking should be viewed as a temporary measure. These stakes should be removed as soon as the tree is able to stand on its own.

Make support stakes just high enough to hold the tree upright under calm conditions; the tree should return to a vertical position after bending in the wind (see illustration).

Support stakes usually are required through the first season. Check deciduous trees to see if they can stand alone at the beginning of the dormant season (the end of autumn), but don't remove the ties until growth begins in the spring. Leave the ties on in the interim to prevent the tree from being broken by winter storms.

The tree should be firmly established

Staking to support the trunk

Two stakes will reduce the likelihood of rubbing injury and uneven trunk development that may occur with one stake.

Ties should be within 2" of the stake top.

Rustproof tacks or staples.

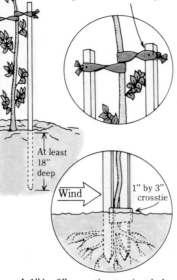

Tie the trunk to the stakes at only one level. The tie should provide some flexibility but not enough that the tree rubs against the stakes.

At least 18" deep

Wind

1" by 3" crosstie

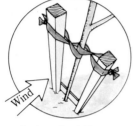

Stakes should be at a right angle to the most troublsome wind.

A 1" by 3" crosstie at or just below ground level will help hold the stake assembly upright and keep it from working out of the ground in the wind.

Polyethylene tape holds trunk to wire.

Wrap the top of wire with tape.

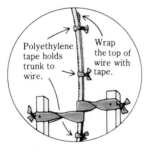

An exceptionally spindly trunk may benefit from an auxiliary stake of spring-steel wire. It adds strength, yet allows flexibility.

Remove the auxiliary stake as soon as possible—usually by the end of the first growing season.

Staking to anchor roots

2 or 3 short stakes will probably be sufficient to anchor the roots. Tie them to the trunk with loops of webbing or plastic tape.

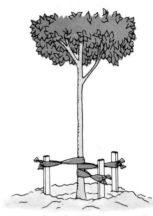

In most cases ties should be removed after the first growing season, when roots have grown securely into the surrounding soil.

A larger tree, when transplanted, may need stronger anchoring until the roots secure it into the surrounding soil.

Attach guy wires to a soft collar around the trunk or to screw eyes. Use a compression spring on each wire for greater flexibility.

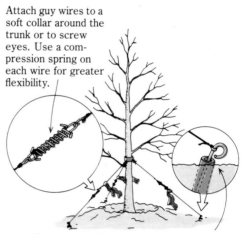

Guy wires with pins that insert into buried pipes can be removed for lawn mowing.

Tie rags to the wires to make them easily visible.

---

by the the end of the second season. If it isn't, investigate the following possibilities: Does the top need to be thinned to reduce weight and wind-resistance? Do the lower branches need to be pinched to encourage additional side growth that will nourish and strengthen the trunk? Has the root system been weakened by circling or kinked roots? If so, you'll have to dig up the tree. Even though it's possible to straighten circling roots and replant the tree, it's better to start with a new tree altogether.

A tree with a spindly trunk and not much trunk taper sometimes needs extra support along most of the lower trunk. A thin, flexible auxiliary stake of spring-

steel wire tied to the trunk will provide the extra strength needed. Spring-steel wire is available in different diameters and various degrees of flexibility. Make the wire just long enough to permit the trunk to return to an upright position after being bent. It should stop at least 2 feet short of the terminal bud of the leader. Tie the auxiliary stake to the trunk with polyethylene tape at 6- to 10-inch intervals. Support stakes are usually needed for another year after the auxiliary stakes have been removed.

Make your own stakes
Either wood (2" × 2") or metal (T-iron) will do for protective anchor or support

stakes. Treat wood with nontoxic preservative (copper sulfate base, not pentachlorophenol) to keep it from rotting. Metal stakes need a flange or plate just below the ground for extra stability.

Ties can be almost any soft, flexible material. Green or black ¼-inch polyethylene tape is probably the least obtrusive. *Don't* use thin materials such as fishing line, twine, or worst of all, wire. Any friction will cause these materials to cut deep into the bark, seriously damaging the tree. If you use wire to guy a tree, loop the wire through a soft collar, such as old garden hose, to protect the trunk of the tree and to prevent girdling. (See illustration.)

Watering and feeding

Trees are able to stand upright because their roots are firmly anchored in soil. The soil holds water and nutrients essential for tree growth. Soil texture, structure, and depth (see page 24) are extremely important to trees throughout their lives.

Clay particles have the ability to become grouped together in aggregates so that each aggregate acts as a single, larger-sized particle. This aggregation is referred to as structure. Well-aggregated soils have the desirable properties of sand (such as good water movement and aeration) as well as the high water- and nutrient-holding capacities of clay. Soils that are primarily sand or silt (intermediate in size) aggregate poorly, so their properties depend essentially on their texture.

Water requirements

All plants require water for growth. They get water from the soil and lose most of it through their leaves by evaporation (transpiration). Plants receive water from either rain or irrigation. How much water is available to a plant depends on the depth and spread of the roots. Most roots are located within three feet of the surface. When there is sufficient water, most of it is supplied from the top three to four feet of soil. In dry periods, deep-rooted plants can draw water from lower roots.

During dry periods, or in areas where irrigation is a necessity, keep a close eye on your trees to determine when they need water. Signs of water stress include wilting, a change in leaf color (from shiny to dull, or from dark green to gray green), and premature leaf fall.

There are a number of ways to water efficiently: basins, furrows, sprinklers, soakers, or drip systems (see illustration). The most important goals are to eliminate run-off, to confine water inside the drip line of branches, and to apply water uniformly. The purpose is to make as much of the applied water available to the tree as possible.

Don't forget that watering a newly planted tree has its own rules. See "Basins," page 26–27.

Fertilizer Requirements

Nitrogen fertilization makes young trees grow more rapidly and reach landscape size more quickly. However, mature trees may need little or no fertilization as long as they have good leaf color and grow reasonably well. In fact, increased vigor may needlessly increase the size of trees and the density of the leaves. Leaves on the inside of such trees, or plants under them, grow poorly because of heavy shade.

Irrigation

Basin: A shallow basin is an efficient way to hold water for a young, newly planted tree.

Furrows: Rows of trees are easily irrigated using parallel furrows on either side of the trees.

Soaker hose: A couple of turns around a tree distributes water evenly.

Sprinkler: A big advantage is that you can measure the amount of water you put on by measuring its depth in an array of coffee cans. This also gives you a check on distribution evenness.

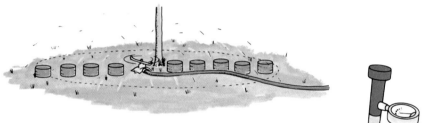

Drip/trickle: To keep trees evenly moist with little wasted water use one of the drip/trickle systems available at your garden center.

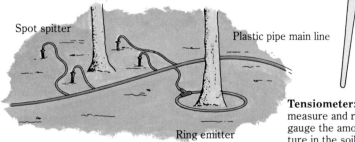

Spot spitter

Plastic pipe main line

Ring emitter

Tensiometer: This lets you measure and read on a gauge the amount of moisture in the soil. Several styles and sizes are available.

As a starter, apply nitrogen at a rate of 2 to 4 pounds per 1,000 square feet. If you are not using a straight nitrogen fertilizer (ammonium nitrate, ammonium sulfate, calcium nitrate, or urea), a so-called "complete" fertilizer (containing nitrogen, phosphorus, and potassium) is fine. Read directions and adjust pounds used according to the percentage of nitrogen in the particular fertilizer. If it's 20 percent, as in 20-4-4, use five times the recommendation.

Another way to figure how much to apply is to measure the diameter of the tree trunk. For each inch, use .1 to .2 pounds of actual nitrogen—in other words, 1 to 2 pounds of a 10 percent nitrogen fertilizer such as 10-8-7.

Because nitrogen is transient, apply the necessary amount at two intervals. One-half in spring and the other half in summer is a good program.

Keep the fertilizer at least 6 inches away from the trunk to avoid injuring the tree. After the first year, apply nitrogen fertilizer to an area with a radius of 1¼ times that of the tree canopy. After application, sprinkle-irrigate the area to wash the fertilizer into the soil. This begins the conversion of the less soluble forms of nitrogen, and avoids burning the grass if the tree is planted in a lawn.

How much fertilizer should you apply? Let the trees be your guide. If growth is excessive on young trees, put on less per area next time or skip a year. If shoot growth is shorter than you want and leaf color is pale, double the rate. As trees mature, fertilize them only if growth or leaf color is not up to expectation.

In most soils you will not need to be concerned about the acidity or alkalinity of the soil. Most trees grow satisfactorily over a wide range of soil reaction. Well-drained soils in high-rainfall areas usually are acid, while poorly drained soils and those in areas of low rainfall are neutral or alkaline. In many alkaline soils, a number of trees may be low in iron, as evidenced by their pale yellow leaves with fine darker green veins. These symptoms are most obvious on the first growth during spring.

An acid-forming nitrogen fertilizer, such as ammonium sulfate, will help make the soil more acid. If symptoms are severe, you can work soil sulfur into the surface soil at about 10 to 20 pounds per 1,000 square feet. More expensive iron chelates are quicker acting and more certain, although the correction may last only one or two seasons. Apply chelates as directed on the label. In areas with alkaline soils, you may want to avoid those species that are most likely to show iron deficiency.

If a tree isn't responding to nitrogen, show or describe the symptoms to experts at your nursery or to your County Extension Agent.

Mulching

A mulch is any material that is put on the soil to cover and protect it. Straw, leaves, wood chips, gravel, and plastic all make effective mulches.

Mulches do many things. They reduce moisture loss, improve soil structure reduce soil erosion, reduce soil compaction, keep weeds down, moderate soil temperatures, and provide a clean, firm surface for walking on during rainy weather.

Most mulches are organic and are the by-product of industry, agriculture, or your own gardening. Some organic mulches are wood shavings, wood chips, twigs, bark, sawdust, leaves, grass, straw, peat moss, rice hulls, corn cobs, cocoa hulls, and pomace. Inorganic mulches include plastic, gravel, crushed brick, and rock.

Prepare the area for mulching by bringing the soil to uniform grade and removing weeds. Apply mulches 3 to 5 inches thick. Keep mulch 6 inches from trunks.

Placing medium-sized gravel, coarse sand, or cinders between the trunk and the mulch will keep both the mulch and hungry rodents away from the trunk.

A single sheet of black plastic eliminates the need for further weed control, but it reduces oxygen penetration and slows the tree's growth. Cut holes in the plastic so that water and oxygen can penetrate to the tree roots. You can improve its appearance by covering it with an organic mulch or crushed rock.

Pruning

Trees grow in many and varied forms. Some develop spreading crowns. Others have central leaders with tall, straight trunks. Intermediate forms can be found between these extremes. The natural characteristics of different kinds of trees should be emphasized through landscape use and maintenance practices. Pruning can do much to enhance tree health and appearance.

Pruning is useful for a number of reasons. Pruning at planting time compensates for root loss of bare-root plants and improves water balance of container-grown trees. Strong branch structure and handsome form can be encouraged. Removing dead wood and crossed branches, and letting light into the interior of the tree will improve its health and appearance. Pruning is particularly useful for controlling tree size. On mature trees, pruning helps to maintain balance between vegetative growth and flowering. Stagnated trees may be brought back to life by severe pruning.

Basic pruning cuts

Cutting at an angle or with the blade moving up takes less effort

Cut up whenever possible. For a close cut, place the blade next to the trunk. When the hook won't fit into the crotch, cut from the side.

Pruning with a saw

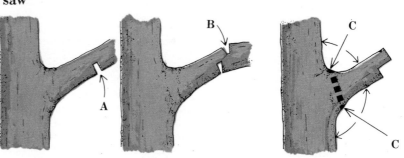

Proper pruning cut   Improper cuts

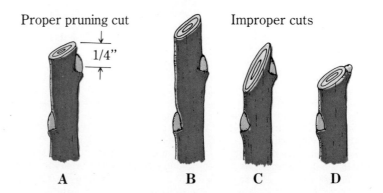

When possible, cut back to a side bud. A proper cut (A) is at an angle about 1/4" above the bud. Improper cuts are: (B) too far from bud, (C) too sharp an angle, and (D) too close to the bud.

Pruning spring-flowering trees

Pruning summer-flowering trees

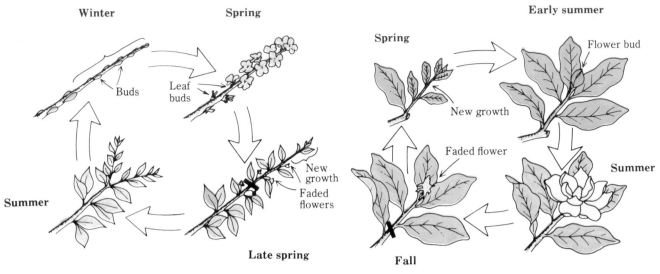

Plants flowering in the spring from buds on 1-year-old wood, especially the flowering fruit trees, should be pruned at or near the end of the bloom period. If you prune in fall or winter you will remove buds that would flower the next spring.

Prune summer-flowering trees in late fall to early spring before growth starts. Pruning new growth removes shoots on which flowers may develop.

Responses to pruning

Pruning is the removal of any portion of a plant. Removing large amounts of healthy growth affects a tree in two seemingly opposite ways. The most obvious response is invigoration. The harder to determine effect is dwarfing.

Removing leafy shoots and buds that would become leaves allows the roots (which are not immediately affected) to supply the remaining parts of the tree with relatively more water and nutrients than before. Shoots are stimulated into growing more rapidly and later into the season. Leaves become larger and darker green, just as if the tree had been fertilized.

Even though leaves will be larger and shoots longer, the total amount of leaf area and new growth will be less on a pruned tree. Because there will be fewer leaves working for a shorter time, less total growth will be made and less food will be stored.

The amount of both invigoration and dwarfing depends on the severity of the pruning. Removing dead, weak, and heavily shaded branches has little influence on growth, while pruning off healthy branches that are well exposed to light can have a significant effect.

Severe pruning can have different effects not only on two different trees, but also on various parts of the same tree. If you wish to subdue a branch within a tree, prune it more severely to reduce its total growth relative to other branches you wish to encourage. Conversely, to encourage a branch to grow more, prune it lightly or not at all. At the same time, prune other branches more severely,

particularly those that might shade or compete with the branch you are trying to encourage. This is the principal way to influence trees to grow the way you want them to grow.

For every generalization, there are always one or more exceptions. For this one there are two: Mature plants that are expected to set a heavy flower and fruit load may not be dwarfed by pruning. In this case, pruning stimulates the remaining shoots, while the number of flowers and fruits on them remain the same. The other exception is the response to pruning by a stagnated young plant. For some unexplained reason, some young trees that are doing poorly but show no symptoms other than lack of vigor will respond with renewed vitality to extremely severe pruning. This usually is a kill-or-cure procedure, however.

The type of pruning determines the tree's response

"Heading" or "heading back" means cutting back to a stub, a lateral bud, or a small lateral branch. New growth comes from one or more buds near the cut; the lower buds don't ordinarily grow. The new shoots are usually vigorous and upright. The new branches and foliage may form a canopy so thick that lower leaves and plants growing under the tree are shaded out.

When large branches of mature trees are headed, it's called "stubbing."

"Thinning" or "thinning out" means removing a branch at its origin or cutting back to another lateral branch. The new growth follows the tree's natural branching pattern and tends to be more evenly distributed throughout the crown. As the

term suggests, "thinning" leaves the canopy less dense and more open. Because more light penetrates through the leaves, interior foliage and plants under the tree will grow better. A thinned tree also will be less subject to wind damage.

For detailed directions on pruning specific fruit trees for fruit production, see Ortho's *All About Growing Fruits & Berries.*

Conifers do not need to be pruned as much as broad-leaved trees. They are pruned primarily to remove dead wood, to control size and shape (see illustration), or to reduce wind resistance. Most conifers do not have latent buds on wood without foliage; if this wood is cut back to a stub, no new growth follows. Exceptions are yew, arborvitae, hemlock, sequoia, some junipers, and some pines.

Conifers typically have a central leader with branches radiating either at random or in vertical whorls around the trunk. Random-branching conifers—arborvitae, sequoia, and yew, for example—can be sheared or tip-pinched to control size and shape. Whorl-branching species—fir, pine, and spruce, for example—will form closer whorls if new growth is headed back to a bud.

When conifers get within a foot of the size you want, cut the new growth back to 1 inch; the tree will hold to size but become more dense.

To train columnar conifers, cut upright branches back to short, spreading laterals; or, in large specimens, head widely spreading branches just inside the desired foliage line of the column.

Lost leaders on conifers can be replaced (see illustration).

Pruning conifers

To make pines more compact and control size, cut off some of each "candle" in late spring to lessen the distance between whorls.

Reduce open spaces in spruce by trimming half of the terminal shoots in the spring when new needles are forming.

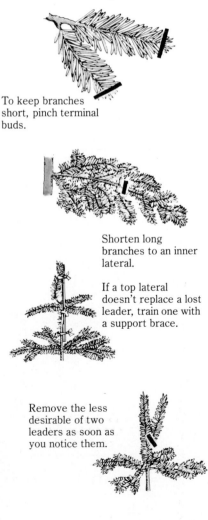

To keep branches short, pinch terminal buds.

Shorten long branches to an inner lateral.

If a top lateral doesn't replace a lost leader, train one with a support brace.

Remove the less desirable of two leaders as soon as you notice them.

The pruning process

Before you pick up your pruning shears, take a moment to get a mental image of what the pruned tree should look like. Then start pruning, in this order:

First, prune away any dead, diseased, or criss-crossing branches.

Then go for form. Make the smallest cuts first, and the largest ones last. Use pruning shears for cutting small limbs (up to an inch or so in diameter). Shears come in a variety of sizes and styles.

Small stems and shoots. With pruning shears, cut away the unwanted growth, cutting just above a healthy lateral bud. Cut ¼ inch above the bud from which you want a branch to grow—more will leave a dead stub, less may damage the bud. It's easier to make a close cut if you place the shears so that the blade cuts upward. Slant the cut upward toward the top of the bud, with the angle in the direction you want the new branch to grow.

Small branches. Branches up to 1¼ inches should be pruned with lopping shears. Again, cut upward. Not only does this make the cutting process easier, it also reduces the danger of bark tearing as the limb falls. Small limbs, including suckers and water sprouts, should be cut as closely to the trunk or branch as possible. This diminishes the chances of new ones sprouting from latent buds left at the base. (Suckers are vigorous sprouts that grow from below the graft union or the ground; water sprouts are similar, but they arise higher on the trunk.) Both grow quite vertically.

Larger branches. A hand or chain saw will work on any branch larger than 1¼ inches. If a branch is too heavy to support with your free hand, first make a rough cut about 6 inches from the trunk, then cut the stub off next to the trunk. This precaution keeps the bark from being stripped off the tree should the heavy branch slip from your hand while you're still cutting. For branches over 3 to 4 inches thick, use a wide-blade, single-edged saw or a chain saw. A 3-legged pruning ladder helps you reach high branches (for extra stability, tie its top to a nearby branch). The best way is to make three cuts (see illustration on page 31).

1. Trim off the side branches. Then make a shallow cut at the underside of the limb about 3 or 4 feet from where it attaches to the trunk.

2. Make a second cut at the upper side of the branch, about 6 inches past the first cut. The limb will then fall away without tearing the bark.

3. Make a third cut where the limb attaches to the trunk, at the "shoulder rings" (or, if you can't find these rings, cut from the top angle of attachment to the bottom angle of attachment).

Structural strength

Certain branch characteristics contribute to the structural strength of the trunk and the major limbs, which are called "scaffolds."

Angle of attachment. Branches that are attached to the tree at a wide angle (45 to 90 degrees) are stronger than those attached at narrower angles. A wide angle allows strong connective wood to form in the crotches, on the sides, and on the lower portion of the branch.

Some narrow-angle branches (less than 45 degrees) are stronger than others. This occurs when the wood of the trunk and branch are joined in the crotch, creating a rough ridge of bark (see illustration). Branches so attached are

Branch attachment strength

A wide angle is strong; a narrow angle with bark ridge, fairly strong; a narrow angle with bark imbedded in the wood is weak.

A narrow-angle branch, although weak, may not break until the branch is quite large.

Most broadleaved plants have more than one bud at a node. But, unless growth is quite vigorous, only one develops. The first bud that grows may have a sharp angle of attachment (left). A wider angle is usually formed from the second bud if the shoot from the first bud is removed (right side).

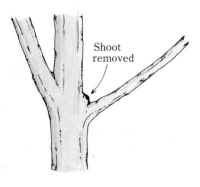

Shoot removed

Branch strength

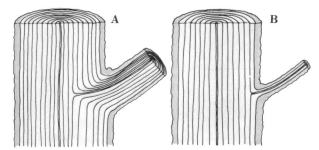
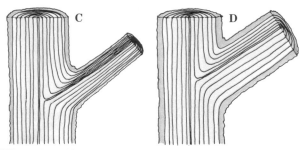

Laterals that grow from a branch or trunk for several years are deeply attached and stong (A). New shoots forced on older limbs are attached only by a thin layer of new wood (B) and can break off easily. These will become stronger as the tree grows.

When a lateral is smaller than the branch or trunk from which it grows (C) it is relatively stronger than the one that is the same size or larger (D).

stronger than those that have attachments with narrow angles, in which the trunk and branch surfaces form a sharp "V." In these, the bark becomes embedded and new wood on top or inside of the crotch is not strongly attached to the trunk. These latter branches may not be a problem until the tree is older; then the branches may break. Such losses not only deform the tree, they are also dangerous. In training a young tree, do not select a narrow-angle branch to be a main scaffold branch.

Relative branch size. This factor also is important in the strength of branch attachments. Branches should be smaller than the trunk or branch they're growing on. Wherever two branches fork, the supporting branch should be larger than the other.

If the branch is too large in relation to the trunk, remove some of its leaves so it will grow more slowly. If the branch has laterals, cut it back to one of these laterals. Both removing the leaves and "heading back" the branch will slow its growth until the supporting branch is larger.

Branches get stronger as they get older, if the original angle of growth is good. New shoots from older wood, whether off the trunk or another branch, are held only by a thin layer of new wood, and are susceptible to breaking easily. They need to develop slowly to reduce the likelihood of breakage.

Training a young tree

Before pruning, decide how you want a tree to function in the landscape. Are you framing an attractive view or screening out a supermarket? Do you want low branches so children can climb the tree, or a high canopy to shade the house? Mature trees can be pruned to suit a particular landscape use, but it is preferable to start with a young tree. Two things determine how a tree should be pruned to the shape you want—the landscape use and the growth habit of the tree. Weak branch attachments may need correcting, and the natural tree form may be accentuated into a living sculpture.

Trees should be pruned only enough to direct their growth effectively and to correct any structural weaknesses. Branches selected for permanent scaffolds (the large branches that give the tree its shape) should have wide angles of attachment.

The height of the first permanent branch will depend on the tree's function in the landscape. The position of a branch of the trunk remains the same throughout the life of the tree. But as a branch increases in diameter, the distance to the ground actually becomes less.

Maintaining a leader

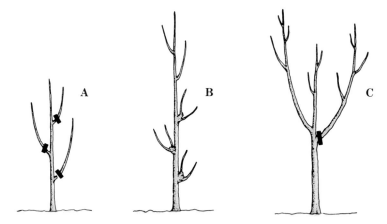

To keep the leader dominant, pinch back strong, competing laterals (A). This creates a well-shaped tree (B). The leader on the right (C) has been choked out by strong growing laterals. The original leader and the less desirable lateral should be removed.

Temporary branches

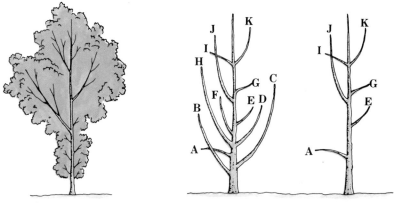

Low, temporary branches protect and nourish the trunks of young trees. Keep them relatively small by pruning.

Selection of temporary branches: Thin out low, vigorous ones (B, C, H); head back low limbs of moderate vigor (D, F), to 2 or 3 buds; leave low, weak twigs (A, E, G, I) and branches suitable for scaffolds (J, K) unpruned.

Vertical branch spacing

The spacing of vertical branches can determine both structural strength and the shape of the tree. Unpruned trees of many species often have the more vigorous branches naturally well spaced, requiring little or no pruning. The distance between branches should be greater on a tree that will mature into a large specimen. Major scaffold branches should be spaced at least 8 inches apart, preferably 18 to 24 inches. Scaffolds that are too close together will have fewer laterals, resulting in long thin branches with little structural strength.

Radial branch distribution should have 5 to 7 scaffolds along the trunk. To accomplish this, make one or two rotations around the trunk, like an ascending spiral. A perfect spiral is not necessary for the tree to be well shaped and for the branches to be healthy and strong. The purpose is to prevent one branch from growing directly over another to the detriment of both—the upper one suffers from the extra competition for water and nutrients, and the lower one gets shaded out. Remove the less desirable branch of the two.

Direct growth during the growing season

During the growing season, pruning can often be done with just a little judicious pinching. Pinch the leader to force more laterals, or pinch back laterals that threaten to dominate the leader. Pinch back, or off, shoots that are too low, too close together, or in competition with branches you want to encourage. Pinching as little as 1 or 2 inches is enough to check growth so that selected limbs will develop properly. There will be little or no setback to the tree if this pinching is done before the shoots are five inches long. It also reduces the necessity of removing large branches later. Growth will be channeled where you want it.

On a young tree, leave more shoots than you ultimately will select as permanent branches. After the second growing season, you will be able to choose from more developed branches.

If your tree is a species that doesn't branch on current growth, you can induce branching by pinching the leader at the height at which you want the first branch. On a vigorous tree, pinching the new shoots will give you as many as three well-spaced branches in one season, instead of a tall, unbranched whip.

Small, temporary branches along the trunk help strengthen the tree and protect it from sunburn. To prevent this, keep some temporary branches along the trunk, particularly on the south side; these shoots will shade the trunk. More important, shoots along the trunk will increase its diameter and taper, resulting in increased strength and flexibility.

Branch structure

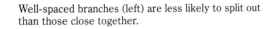

A tree with evenly spaced, well-developed laterals needs little or no pruning unless some limbs are too low.

Well-spaced branches (left) are less likely to split out than those close together.

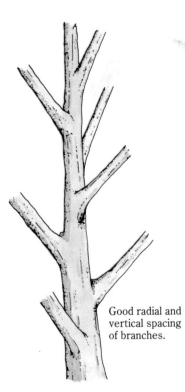

Good radial and vertical spacing of branches.

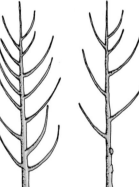

When one limb is directly over another, each interferes with the proper development of the other. Remove one of them.

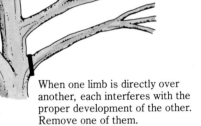

When thinning a young tree, leave more scaffold branches than eventually will be needed. As the tree grows you can select those that will be the most desirable permanent branches.

Inducing lateral branches

A non-branching leader can be pinched during the growing season to induce the development of laterals. Two pinches, over two seasons, can produce branches at the height desired. Leaves have been left off the drawing for clarity.

Regaining a leader

When a leader has lost its dominance, prune it back to a newly selected leader.

Heading a weak tree

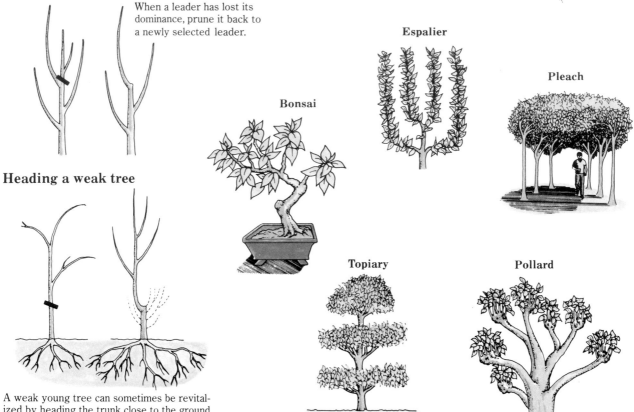

A weak young tree can sometimes be revitalized by heading the trunk close to the ground (about 6 inches) or the graft union. Select a new leader from the strongest of the new shoots.

Pruning specialties

Espalier

Bonsai

Pleach

Topiary

Pollard

Temporary branches should be about 4 to 12 inches apart, and should be kept short by pinching. This is one place where you want weak growth. Choose the less vigorous shoots along the trunk for temporary branches.

As the young tree develops a sturdy trunk and permanent branches that shade the trunk, the temporary branches can be reduced and eventually eliminated. You can begin reducing their number after two or three years, when the trunk is 2 to 3 inches in diameter for small trees, 5 to 6 inches for trees that will get larger. Remove them over a period of two to three years, each time pruning out the largest ones.

Sometimes the tree you buy will have been headed at the nursery. Such trees will have several branches close together, coming from below the cut. For many landscape uses, however, these branches will be too low. Try to find a tree with well-spaced branches.

Upright branches usually are more vigorous than horizontal branches. If an upright branch is in a good position for a permanent branch, it will grow well and hold its own in competition with other branches. If the upright branch threatens the leader, select a more horizontal branch, or reduce the size of the upright one. This is mainly a concern with a young tree—as a tree matures, the

leader often loses control and the tree becomes more spreading.

Prevailing winds can deform trees. Most of the growth may be on the downwind side. Depending on wind conditions and the kind of tree, the main leader may or may not be bent. Many trees can stand upright under strong prevailing winds, while others are easily modified by wind.

In certain situations, you may like the picturesque form sculpted by the wind. If not, thin out the top of the tree by removing moderate-sized branches. The tree will offer less wind resistance.

Sometimes a leader loses its control and is overtaken by one or more upright laterals. If the leader cannot be saved without severe pruning, choose the lateral in the best position and thin the leader back to it. Other laterals may need to be pruned to be sure the new leader will dominate.

Because pruning forces new growth, severe pruning is sometimes used as a last ditch effort to revitalize a weak-growing, stagnated tree. Before deciding on this method, make sure there's no other problem that needs correction—poorly drained soil, insect infestation, disease, girdled roots. All these conditions weaken a tree and will not be improved by pruning. If nothing else seems to be wrong, take a deep breath and cut the tree to within 6 to 12 inches of the

ground (or graft union). When new growth breaks from latent buds, choose the strongest upright shoot to be the new leader and cut back the other shoots. There are a few species that will not respond: Test by cutting back a branch and watching to see if it resprouts.

You can use your knowledge of how plants respond to pruning to accentuate the natural form of trees, or even to modify them into almost any form you desire. Guying, staking, tying, and twisting can be used along with pruning to direct tree growth. Trees can be thinned to better display branching and interesting bark patterns, as well as to let sunlight dapple the interior of the trees and the landscape below.

A number of pruning specialties are illustrated on this page. Some are quite useful. Weather-wise gardeners know the importance of protecting fruit trees by planting them against warm walls.

Pruning mature trees

A tree's scaffold limbs and its main structure have usually been selected by the third or fourth year, depending on the kind of tree and its growing conditions. If the scaffolds are well placed, the tree may need little or no pruning for several years.

There are several reasons why mature trees may need to be pruned.

Tree health and appearance can be improved by removing limbs that are dead, weak, diseased, or insect-infested. Remove broken, low, and crossing limbs for appearance and safety.

The structural features of a tree may be emphasized by moderate thinning to open the tree to view. This turns just another tree into an attractive feature.

To open up a medium to large-sized tree (40 to 60 feet), make moderate-sized (1–2 inches in diameter) thinning cuts of limbs. For smaller trees, somewhat smaller cuts are appropriate. These should be made around the tops and sides of the tree. Remove branches that are close to others. In some larger trees, cuts may remove limbs up to 6 inches in diameter. However, such larger cuts indicate that the tree has not been properly pruned in the past, or that its use in the landscape has changed.

Most people delay pruning large trees in the home landscape for as long as possible. This is because the need is not easy to recognize—and when it is, you may not be sure who should do the job or how much it costs to have it done. Even if you do know what to do, the trees usually are so large that you have neither the equipment nor the experience to prune safely.

If you plan to have an arborist prune your trees, choose one carefully. It isn't easy to recognize the work of a skilled arborist unless you see the pruning actu-ally being done. Severe stubbing often is thought to be "the way to prune." In some cases, such heavy heading may be the only alternative, but (as the illustrations show) there also are other ways. Trees can be reduced in size and poor structure can be improved by proper thinning. Be sure you know what the arborist is going to do before pruning begins. Your local nursery or garden center may be able to recommend a responsible arborist.

Pruning mature trees

Thinning opens up a mature tree while retaining its natural form and appearance (center). You can hold or reduce the height as desired. A headed tree (right) will force many weakly attached, vigorous upright shoots, destroying the tree's natural form.

When you wish to remove one (or more) of a group of trees which has become crowded, prune the expendable tree back more severely each year for several years until ready to remove. This will allow proper development of the remaining trees while retaining the value of the temporary tree.

Winter chilling—rest

Although all trees will die if the weather gets cold enough, many trees native to temperate regions require a certain amount of winter cold in order to start growth satisfactorily in the spring. This is particularly true of fruit trees, which need cold in order to flower and fruit successfully. In a number of fruit-growing areas, winters are not cold enough for the profitable production of some kinds of fruit.

As the days of summer begin to shorten, the buds of many temperate-zone trees and shrubs begin to enter a condition called "rest." In this situation, they will not grow even though conditions are favorable. This is nature's excellent scheme to keep a tree from beginning to grow during warm spells in winter, only to be damaged by fatally low temperatures soon afterwards.

However, rest can be a problem if trees are grown in areas where the winters are not cold enough to overcome or satisfy the rest. When this happens, trees are slow to leaf out and bloom is delayed. Leaf buds are affected more seriously than flower buds. In extreme cases, so few buds grow that branches are sunburned and the tree is weakened because of lack of carbohydrates. Since flower buds are less affected, a tree may bloom and set fruit. This, however, just weakens the tree further.

To rest, buds must be exposed to low temperatures, usually below 45°F, for 4 to 8 weeks. As might be expected, different species and different varieties or selections within a species require different durations of temperatures below 45°F to overcome rest.

The rest period of the roots of some woody plants depends on their tops. However, roots of most species seem to grow whenever food reserves and soil conditions are favorable. The roots of most trees will grow at lower temperatures than the shoots. For example, roots of silver maple will start growth at 40°F but leaf buds do not expand until the temperature is at least 50°F for 20 days. This is one reason why it is important to plant in the fall, in areas where the ground does not freeze: Roots can grow in soil that remains warm while the air begins to cool.

Tree insects and disease

That often-used word—stress—is frequently the key to insect and disease problems in trees. Proper care will do much to reduce tree problems.

But often even if several stress factors can be reduced, a tree will still be affected by some insect pest or disease organism. If this happens to you, you have the option of calling in a professional arborist or handling the problem yourself. There are advantages to treating the problems yourself—you are more familiar with your trees, if for no other reason than that you probably walk through your garden each day. Early detection of such problems and proper timing of sprays are valuable tools against the tree pests.

The older and larger trees become, the more difficult they are to treat yourself. Ideally, that is the time to call a professional arborist.

The following are some common tree pests and control methods. Spraying is not always recommended treatment; but when it is, read and follow the directions on the label. This will benefit your tree, yourself, and your neighbors.

Anthracnose. This general term refers to many different fungi that affect maple, ash, sycamore, oak, and linden trees, among others. The fungi usually attack leaves and produce small brown spots that may coalesce, giving a scorched appearance to the entire leaf. Then the leaf drops. Usually, young leaves are attacked, particularly in a wet spring. "Witch's brooms" (groups of brushlike, weak stems) often develop because of the repeated cycle of defoliation, followed by a second crop of leaves. Anthracnose weakens trees and is particularly serious after several consecutive wet springs.

CONTROL: Apply fungicides maneb and zineb when buds are first opening. Trees should also be well fertilized and growing vigorously.

Beetles. There are many leaf-eating beetles. Two of the most destructive are the elm leaf beetle and the Japanese beetle. Elm leaf beetles skeletonize leaves. Infested elms can be completely defoliated—a devitalizing process that invites borers.

The Japanese beetle (presently not a problem in the West) is a ½-inch, metallic green beetle with a coppery back. These beetles damage many trees severely, usually by eating the entire leaf between the veins, thus skeletonizing it.

CONTROL: Spray with carbaryl when the the damage is first noticed, and repeat as necessary. Be sure to read the label. You can also apply Orthene® to control elm leaf beetle.

Borers. Any tree that is in a weakened—stressed—condition will attract borers. Drought, sun scald, frost cracks, poor soil, bark injury, and air pollution are some of the major causes of stress and, consequently, of borer attack. Damage includes structural weakening, death by girdling the cambium layer, and vulnerability to disease organisms. Holes in the bark indicating the presence of borers may be very tiny or up to one inch in diameter; they may be round or oval.

CONTROL: First, do everything possible to reduce stress and keep the tree in good health. Only long residual types of insecticides, such as lindane, are commonly used against borers. Timing is very important. Read the label. Commercial tree wraps are available and can stop borers from infesting the tree.

Cankers. This word describes dead and diseased areas that develop, usually on woody branches or trunks. A common symptom is die-back starting at branch tips. Virtually all plants can be attacked by canker-forming diseases.

CONTROL: Prune and burn dead and infected branches. Paint pruning wounds with a disinfectant. When trunks are seriously invaded, often the tree cannot be saved.

Some cankers "bleed." Maples, elms, birch, and low-vigor trees are particularly susceptible.

To best control bleeding cankers, restore the tree's vigor by supplying proper water and fertilizer. Control insects and prune to thin in late winter when bleeding is reduced. Then clean the wound back to healthy bark so callus can form.

Caterpillars. Moths and butterflies are harmless creatures, but their larva—tent caterpillars, bagworms, and loopers, to name just a few—are some of the most damaging leaf-chewing pests. At first they are small and feeding damage is light. When full-size, however, they are ravenous and can defoliate entire trees.

CONTROL: Contact insecticides, such as carboryl and diazinon, are effective against these pests. So is the systemic Orthene®. Read the label.

Honeydew. Some insects that feed on trees by sucking their sap excrete honeydew, a sticky, clear, sugary material. Large numbers of ants, flies, and even honeybees are early symptoms of the presence of these insects. (The famous Black Forest honey is made by honeybees from honeydew.) In time, a black sooty mold will grow on the honeydew,

Anthracnose on sycamore.

Elm leaf beetle.

Borers on a pine.

A canker.

Gypsy moth caterpillars on oak.

Sooty mold on honeydew on a leaf.

often blackening the leaves of infested plants. Aphids, soft scales, and leaf hoppers are often responsible for honeydew.

CONTROL: In winter, use a dormant oil spray to control overwintering eggs of many pests, including honeydew excreting insects. In summer, use the systemic Orthene®, or contact insecticides such as diazinon and malathion. In all cases, read the label.

Fireblight. This is a bacterial disease that affects many plants of the rose family, including crabapples, hawthorn, loquat, and mountain ash.

CONTROL: See *Malus* in the encyclopedia section for description and control of fireblight.

Powdery mildew. Powdery mildew is a fungus disease that causes a grayish, powdery coating to form on young shoots, leaves, and flower buds. It can deform or kill them. Powdery mildew thrives where air circulation is poor, and it grows best in shade. Many shade and flowering trees are attacked by this disease.

CONTROL: Use a fungicide labelled to control this disease.

Scales. These are small, sucking insects—the largest is less than ⅜ of an inch in diameter. Scales are largely immobile except when in the "Crawler" stage, which usually occurs in the spring, after the eggs hatch. There are many

scales that damage trees. If left unchecked, scales can build up large populations that weaken and even kill trees.

CONTROL: A dormant oil spray in winter smothers scales or their overwintering eggs with a thin layer of oil. When applying dormant oil sprays, read the label carefully and follow directions literally. During the summer, watch for tiny, crawling insects (the scale crawlers) to appear, then spray with Orthene®, diazinon, or malathion.

The major insect and disease problems are discussed throughout the encyclopedia section of this book (pages 59–108). For additional information on the control of pests and diseases, check with your local County Extension Agent.

Fireblight on a crabapple.

Powdery mildew on a sycamore leaf.

Cottony maple scale.

WHICH TREES

Which trees are right for your neighborhood? Which trees deserve special care? Which trees are best suited to your climate? When you select a tree, each of these questions is important and each must be answered in turn.

Liking a tree and successfully growing that tree may be two different things. It isn't always immediately apparent which trees will do well where, and it's no favor to you, the tree, or your neighborhood to plant the right tree in the wrong place. So how can you make a good match? This chapter is filled with that information and will give you some good, solid ideas.

Tree climates

The most important aspect of selecting a tree is its cold tolerance. All trees have a minimum temperature that they can survive. If the thermometer drops below this number, the tree will often die. Some trees also have a limit to the amount of heat they can withstand, and they should not be grown in areas where the temperatures consistently rise above this limit.

The map on pages 46 and 47 is divided into ten plant hardiness zones and each tree listed in this book is described in terms of which of these zones it will grow in.

The zoning information given is from the United States Department of Agriculture (USDA). It is a simple system in which the country is divided into climate zones that are described by the lowest recorded winter temperatures.

According to the USDA map, zones change from north to south only by minimum temperatures; but be aware that these zones are meant to be a general guide and tree climates often vary within zones. There are a number of reasons for this: Large bodies of water, snowcover, soil types, slope of the land, elevation, and air drainage all will influence tree

climates. If you have any question about the hardiness of the tree you wish to plant, be sure to check with your local nursery or County Extension Agent.

General climate considerations

South- and west-facing slopes are always warmer than north and east slopes because they absorb more of the sun's radiant energy. Therefore they affect cold-tender plants and those that grow best on hot, sunny sites. Thermal belts are warm microclimates that develop on sloping land above valleys and other lowlands. These bands of mild temperatures

are localized; both above and below them, winters are distinctly colder. Therefore, if your garden is in a warm thermal belt, you probably will be able to grow a number of plants considered too cold-tender for the general area.

Structural walls, plant hedges, and screens can act as a dam and can create a frost pocket by trapping cold air on the uphill side. If these are arranged to deflect the downhill flow of cold air around gardens and outdoor living areas, they provide shelter and protection.

Buildings, automobiles, large expanses of concrete, and other heat-absorbing

Elms are hardy throughout the United States. See page 107.

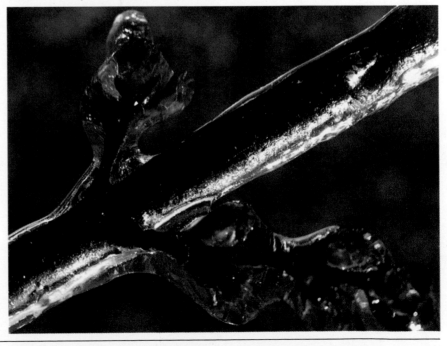

Left: The red maple, *Acer rubrum*, earns its common name in the fall when the leaves turn to vivid shades of magenta and red. The leaf-strewn ground below the tree takes on an abstract design.

surfaces all contribute to making cities and towns warmer than outlying areas. Likewise, the warmest areas in the garden are usually those beside paved surfaces such as sidewalks, driveways, patios, and sunny south and west walls. Not only do these surfaces reflect some of the sun's heat, light, and glare, but they also store heat during daylight hours and radiate it back to the atmosphere at night. Dark surfaces absorb more heat than light-colored ones.

Each side of a building has its own microclimate, which strongly influences plant growth. The cool, shaded, north side is best for cold-tolerant plants and those that do not grow well in full sunlight. A wall that faces south receives maximum sunlight throughout the year; plants that tolerate intense heat and brilliant sunlight do well here. Both east- and west-facing walls are exposed to a half-day of sun, but high afternoon temperatures create a much hotter microclimate against the west wall.

Tree climates of the North

Even in the coldest winter climates, there are ways to work with the weather so that storm damage is reduced and the really low temperatures are foiled. Snow, for example, is the finest mulch against cold. It holds a lot of air and insulates against below-freezing temperatures. Still, the weight of heavy snow can damage evergreen foliage, snapping branches or deforming the shape of the tree. Therefore, knock or shake snow off evergreens whenever you can.

Drought is a major menace in winter when the ground freezes and water can't move down to the roots, so water thoroughly before the ground freezes. Good watering and mulching prevents a lot of cold burn and keeps the roots from heaving out of the ground in freeze-and-thaw cycles.

Wind is the chief menace in winter, especially in the Great Plains. It breaks snow-laden branches, dries exposed branches and foliage, and increases existing cold. Your best answer is a permanent windbreak of hardy trees. A windbreak is effective only if some of the wind can blow straight through. This creates a leeward turbulence, which keeps the main force of the wind up above your garden. Good windbreak trees are listed below:

Botanical name	Common name
Celtis occidentalis	Common hackberry
Elaeagnus angustifola	Russian olive
Juniperus virginiana	Eastern red cedar
Populus nigra 'Italica'	Lombardy poplar
Rhamnus alaternus	Italian buckthorn

Top left: Lombardy poplar is a good choice where winter winds are damaging. Top right: Paper birch are hardy into the Canadian prairies. Bottom: Red oaks are hardy only as far north as the southern Great Lakes.

Great Lakes. The influence of the Great Lakes is complex, resulting in great climate variation between locations on opposite shores. For example, Lake Michigan (like all large bodies of water) responds to temperature changes slowly, delaying the onset of seasonal weather. Predominantly westerly winds sweep across the lake and buffer the eastern shores against extremes.

Autumn tends to be cloudy on eastern shores when moisture-laden air condenses as it moves inland. Thus, Madison, Wisconsin, receives an average of 42 percent sunshine in January, while Lansing, Michigan, receives only 27 percent. Precipitation also varies from east to west. In winter, Milwaukee, Wisconsin, can expect precipitation on the average of every 5 days, while Muskegon, Michigan, averages every other day.

Each lake has its own influence on nearby areas in the United States and Canada. For example, the farther north you go in Ohio toward Lake Erie, the longer the growing season becomes. In Cleveland, along the southern shore, the growing season is 195 days. But away from the lake's influence, in the Ohio River valleys, the season is reduced to as low as 140 days.

Snow cover varies throughout the entire Great Lakes region. Lake influences create what is often called a snow belt, which extends along the eastern and southern portions of the Great Lakes from Chicago to Buffalo and is notorious for high winter snowfall.

Hardiness in the North. Hardiness gets more important the farther north you go. Gregory N. Brown, professor of forestry at the University of Missouri, Columbia, talks about winter hardiness this way:

"Early fall freezes, late spring freezes, and severe freezes during winter months often press trees beyond their limits of survival. Usually a tree can handle freezing weather, when prepared for it—a process referred to as winter hardiness, frost hardiness, cold hardiness, or numerous other names. Trees can read environmental changes such as shortening days and cooler temperatures in the fall. These signals bring about changes in the tree that prepare it for winter. Each tree species has differing capacities to prepare itself for freezing winter weather."

The following trees are listed as extremely hardy (less than −40° C.):

Botanical name	Common name
Betula papyrifera	Paper birch
Picea abies	Norway spruce
Pinus strobus	White pine
Robinia pseudoacacia	Black locust
Ulmus americana	American elm

Tree climates of the South

The South is a large area. It includes the South Atlantic Coast influence, the Gulf Coast, the arid regions of the South, and the cooler northern regions—so variations are the rule in the South.

Great fluctuations in temperature occur when the continental air mass pushes further south than usual. A 60° or 70° F. daytime temperature can plummet to 20° F. or lower during the night.

Growing days (days between frosts) vary from 187 to 365.

Then there's winter chilling: Many northern trees require 1,000 hours or more of winter temperatures below 45 degrees.

In the colder regions, the slope of the land makes a difference, too. Weather varies with the length of a slope, so it matters where you live on that slope. As the air next to the ground cools at night, it becomes heavier. Like water, it slowly flows downhill into washes, valleys, or cold-air basins, filling depressions and low spots as it progresses.

John Ford of the Secrest Arboretum in Wooster, Ohio, has spent many years in the South. He adds these comments on slopes and elevations. The important regions in the Southeast are Coastal Plain, Piedmont, and Mountains.

"In the southern mountains, we find Canadian vegetation at elevations of 5,000 to 6,000 feet—spruce and fir forests. A rough rule of thumb: a thousand feet difference in elevation in the southern mountains is equivalent to going 300 miles further north at the same elevation (depending on exposure). In the southern mountains, one always sleeps under a blanket at night. The days are hot and the nights are cool in summer. At Sylvia, N.C., I had yucca at 1,700 feet and at 2,700 feet. There was a difference of two weeks in the dates of initial bloom. The north slope is always important in the South as far as microclimates are concerned. In Raleigh, N.C., where I lived, the property had a steep north slope, and certain northern hardwoods such as *Quercus rubra*, northern red oak, were growing there naturally. We had loblolly pine (a southern pine) in front of the house on the south slope.

"In general, the north and east slopes in the southern mountains are the best timber-producing sites, especially for northern hardwoods. There is usually more moisture on these slopes. The south and west slopes tend to dry out, and lack of moisture can be a problem.

"Precipitation is quite variable in the South. For example, the annual precipitation varies from 35 inches west of Asheville, N.C., to 82 inches at Highlands, N.C. Over 100 inches has been recorded around Highlands. Close weather stations at Coweeta have indicated 30 to 40 inches difference in a half mile."

The South also has a variety of soil types. Much of the South is in high-rainfall areas, so it has acid soil. The rain washes lime from the soil, gradually increasing its acidity (lowering the pH). If you need to lime your lawn every year, that tells you you're in a high-rainfall, acid-soil area.

In the Southwest, rainfall is low and soils are more alkaline (higher pH). In arid regions, the pecan (which is prone to scab disease in humid areas) commonly develops a zinc deficiency. Zinc might be present in the soil but it is unavailable to the pecan because of the soil's alkalinity.

To illustrate the different climates of the South, we have compared the cities of Atlanta, Georgia; Tulsa, Oklahoma; and Lubbock, Texas.

We checked average minimum temperatures in January and average maximums in July. We also noted the average percent of sunshine in July, inches of rain during the growing season, number of days of rain, and length of the growing season.

Climate comparisons in three cities

	Atlanta	Tulsa	Lubbock
Av. min. temp. (°F.)	31	26	26
Av. max. temp. (°F.)	88	93	92
Percent sunshine	62	76	81
Inches of rain	29	27	15
Days of growing season	244	216	205

These figures tell a story. Atlanta is mild and humid. Many days are overcast, and the growing season is long. Lubbock is drier, sunnier, and colder. Tulsa is in the middle. These three cities demonstrate some of the climate variations in the South.

Tree adaptation is another factor. Just because a tree doesn't suffer frost damage in either Atlanta or Lubbock doesn't necessarily mean that it is well adapted in either city. As John Ford says, "Heat also may be setting up a more favorable climate for tree pests such as insects and disease. This can be a limiting factor in the southward spread of northern trees. One example is red pine and tip moth. Another is mimosa webworm, which is usually more severe on honeylocust in the south than in the North." Texas is a big state and Lubbock represents only one small part of this vast state. Climates vary a great deal from the gulf coast to the cold northern panhandle. The climate of northern Texas produces its famous grapefruits and mesquites. Because of the large area it covers, much of the climate in Texas differs from what we traditionally think of as "Southern."

The Texas State Horticultural Society (Drawer HA, College Station, Texas 77840) recommends the following trees for use in north Texas:

Botanical name	Common name
Ilex vomitoria	Yaupon holly
Magnolia grandiflora	Southern magnolia
Prosopis glandulosa torreyana	Mesquite
Quercus alba	White oak
Taxodium distichum	Bald cypress

The many tropical trees of south Florida and the gulf coast are beyond the scope of this book. However, we do discuss many that are adapted in zone 10. For example, the encyclopedia covers *Eriobotrya japonica*, loquat; *Lagerstroemia indica*, crape myrtle, *Ligustrum lucidum*, glossy privet; *Magnolia grandiflora*, Southern magnolia; and *Nyssa sylvatica*, black tupelo.

Check with your County Extension Agent for performance of these trees: *Bauhinia variegata*, orchid tree; *Brachychiton acerifolius*, flame tree; *Jacaranda acutifolia*, Jacaranda; and *Stenocarpus sinuatus*, firewheel tree.

Black tupelo is a native forest tree of the South. See page 89.

The southern magnolia is a symbol of the South and also a superior lawn tree. See page 86.

Tree climates of the West

All the various "temperate zone" climates are found in the West. They range from harsh winters to moist, ocean-moderated climates, to the deserts of the southwest. The major climate influences are described below.

A climate of cold winters (0–30° F.) and warm summers (80–100° F.) is found where the Columbia and Snake rivers are a major influence and create many warm microclimates. Rainfall varies between 12 and 17 inches per year.

The waters of the Puget Sound, the San Juan Islands, and the Queen Charlotte Sound influence the strip of coastal land along Southern British Columbia, including Vancouver Island, and south along the coast to Crescent City, California. Inland, it is progressively colder. But minimum temperatures range from 28° to 32° F. along this coastal strip. An increase in distance from the water causes winter temperatures to decrease and summer temperatures to increase. This area along the coast is prime rhododendron country.

In Oregon's Willamette Valley, weather stations have not recorded temperatures lower than 16° F. for over half their years of record. However, below-zero temperatures do occur on an average of every 25 years. Air movement is very important. During the December 1972 freeze, lows near Portland were 12° F. Down the Willamette Valley they gradually decreased, until Salem, where the minimum was −10° F. Drying winds out of the Columbia River Gorge can be a problem, but sometimes they help: Poor water drainage can present problems in the valley. Even slopes can suffer from water-logged soil.

The Sacramento and San Joaquin valleys, Redding, Sacramento, Davis, Fresno, and Bakersfield, represent a range of conditions. There is some decreasing marine influence from ocean air-flow entering through the Suisun Straits and the Delta, mainly affecting the western central portion of the Great Valley. Many thermal belts in the southern portion allow commercial citrus orchards above the valley. Growing conditions are greatly modified by water source. High summer temperatures and moderate winters with considerable fog are typical. A wide range of introduced trees can be grown. Crape myrtle, camphor, citrus, and pecans thrive. But high summer heat causes some trees to outgrow themselves—for example the Chinese hackberry, deodar cedar, and Italian stone pine.

The climate of Fort Bragg, San Francisco, and down the coast to Santa Cruz is dominated by the ocean. It has mild winters, low summer temperatures, and summer fog. Subtropicals that require a long warm season will not thrive here. These are ideal conditions for many

California oaks lend their grandeur to the native countryside. See pages 101 and 102.

native trees—among them madrone, bishop pine, coast redwood, bay laurel, and Monterey cypress.

In the Northern California coastal valleys and adjacent area, the climate generally is mild to warm. Extremely hot weather can occur, but not as frequently nor for as long as in the Sacramento and San Joaquin valleys. The winters are generally milder and less foggy than in these areas. Temperatures are modified by the ocean's influence and are slightly warmer in the valleys north of San Francisco. Choose from a wide selection of introduced deciduous and evergreen trees: magnolia, camphor, liquidambar, ginkgo, pistachio, and Canary Island pine are outstanding; as are olive, California pepper, Australian willow, and African sumac. The interior valleys of southern California are little influenced by the Pacific Ocean and there are many microclimates. On hillsides where the cold air is drained, the climate is favorable for subtropicals that can withstand winter cold of 25° F. Higher elevations are colder and have desertlike vegetation.

The thermal belts of southern California, from Vista to Santa Barbara, have the favored climate for the avocado. Deciduous trees that require winter cold do poorly here.

Along the coastal strip of southern California, the area dominated by the ocean, some weather stations have never recorded a freezing temperature. The extent of ocean influence varies considerably.

The climates of China Lake, Ridgecrest, California City, Mojave, Lancaster, Palmdale, Barstow, and Victor-ville make up California's intermediate desert. Common to all is a winter in which temperatures may drop to a cold 6° F for a day or two. The last frost of spring generally comes in March, but an occasional April frost is possible. Between June and September there will be many days of temperatures over 90° F. The nights and mornings are relatively cool. Wind gusts reaching 40 miles an hour are common in spring.

The low desert of California and Arizona is represented by the climates of Phoenix, Palm Springs, Palm Desert, Indio, Brawley, El Centro, Blyth, Yuma, Desert Hot Springs, the Salton Sea area, and Borrego Springs. Temperatures range from the low 20s to 115° F. Heavy winds from March through June are not uncommon. Many of the so-called tropicals will thrive here. Some of the trees that grow locally in this area are Indian laurel, fig, jacaranda, olive, crape myrtle, evergreen ash, evergreen pear, Brazilian pepper, African sumac, and of course, the citrus fruits.

The intermediate desert of Arizona is shared by the cities of Tucson, Wickenburg, Florence, and Safford. The winter temperatures are somewhat lower than the low desert of California and Arizona, and the number of days with temperatures below 32° F. are more numerous. In the Arizona and New Mexico high desert maximum temperatures are lower compared to the low desert. The lowest temperatures are around 8° F., the number of days above 90° F. range from 100 to 150, and the nights are relatively cool. There are many thermal belts in this area. In New Mexico we find Albuquerque partly associated with the desert and partly with the southern Rocky Mountains. Favored trees of this zone are the olive, pomegranate, sweet acacia, pinyon pine, and many natives. This area is represented by the cities of Deming, Coolege, Alamogordo, Roswell, Kingman, Bisbee, Douglas, Globe, and Sedona.

Camphor trees are pest-free and tough, making them a common selection for street trees in the West. See page 71.

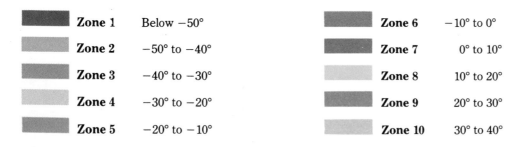

Plant climate zones

These zones are based on mean minimum temperatures, and represent only an *average* for areas within the zone. Your location might be a zone or two warmer than the map shows if you live near a large body of water, or a zone or two colder if you live at a high elevation or on a north-facing slope. Adapted from the USDA Plant Climate Zone Map.

Range of average minimum temperatures for each zone:

Zone 1	Below −50°	
Zone 2	−50° to −40°	
Zone 3	−40° to −30°	
Zone 4	−30° to −20°	
Zone 5	−20° to −10°	

Zone 6	−10° to 0°	
Zone 7	0° to 10°	
Zone 8	10° to 20°	
Zone 9	20° to 30°	
Zone 10	30° to 40°	

Tree guideposts

From the great world of trees, we have chosen a few to serve as a guide. We list some trees by their attributes or characteristics, and others by their functions. Each list is only a fraction of all the trees that could be included in that category. However, these are the choice of the lot.

One tree may fulfill many needs. If you are considering a tree for the patio, for example, also consider it for summer flowers, fall color, winter form, color in more than one season, fruits and berries, fragrant flowers, and interesting bark or leaf shapes. While no one tree will fit all categories, a certain kind of tree may have the characteristics that matter most to you.

Think of trees not as single, isolated plantings but as groupings to solve problems. There are many situations in which trees are very useful. Consider:

- Trees espaliered informally against the west wall of the house provide natural, free air-conditioning.
- Trees can be used as a screen to create privacy if your home is close to the one next door.
- Wall trees add grace to angular walls of apartment houses and condominiums.
- Trees can hide a fence more quickly than most permanent vines.
- Giant trees can be kept smaller by careful pruning (see pages 32 and 33).

- Trees can be miniaturized and kept in pots or tubs for years, if your space is limited.
- Trees can help out problem sites: there are those that will withstand flooding, grow along a coast, or stand up to the harshest city conditions.

Use these lists as your first introduction to the encyclopedic listing of trees in the next chapter.

Zones are listed to guide you, but remember that zoning, at best, is only a generality. Tree performance varies by location. Check with your local nursery or County Extension Agent.

Quick-growing temporary trees

These trees supply quick landscape effect. Some may be considered "weed trees," but they can be interplanted with "desirables" and removed as the slower trees reach functional size.

Botanical name	Common name	Zone
Acacia species	Acacia	9–10
Acer saccharinum	Silver maple	3–7
Albizia julibrissin	Silk tree	7–10
Alnus species	Alder	3–9*
Casuarina cunninghamiana	Beefwood	6–7
Catalpa species	Catalpa	5–10
Eucalyptus species	Eucalyptus	9–10*
Grevillea robusta	Silk oak	10
Paulownia tomentosa	Empress tree	7–10
Populus species	Poplar	2–10*
Robinia pseudoacacia	Black locust	4–9
Salix species	Willow	2–9*
Sapium sebiferum	Chinese tallow tree	8–9
Ulmus species	Elm	3–9*

*Varies with each species. See encyclopedia.

***Catalpa* species**

Malus floribunda

Trees that attract birds

All trees attract birds. However, because these trees provide abundant fruit as well as cover, they attract birds in flocks.

Botanical name	Common name	Zone
Amelanchier canadensis	Serviceberry	4–5
Arbutus species	Madrone	7–9
Cornus species	Dogwood	5–9
Crataegus species	Hawthorn	4–9*
Elaeagnus angustifolia	Russian olive	1–8
Eriobotrya japonica	Loquat	7–9
Ilex species	Holly	6–10*
Juniperus virginiana	Eastern red cedar	3–7
Laurus nobilis	Sweet bay	8–10
Malus species	Crabapple	2–9*
Prunus species	Plums, cherries, cherry laurels	2–10*
Quercus species	Oak	4–9*
Sorbus species	Mountain ash	2–7*

*Varies with each species. See encyclopedia.

Trees that can be miniaturized

Many shrubs and trees can be miniaturized, bonsai style. To dwarf trees naturally, restrict their roots to a small container and prune carefully.

Botanical name	Common name	Zone
Acer species	Maple	3–9*
Cedrus species	Cedar	5–10*
Cercidiphyllum japonicum	Katsura	
Chamaecyparis species	False cypress	4–9*
Cotinus coggygria	Smoke tree	5–9
Fagus sylvatica	European beech	5–10
Ginkgo biloba	Maidenhair tree	5–10
Laurus nobilis	Sweet bay	8–10
Malus species	Crabapple	2–9*
Pinus species	Pine	3–10*
Ulmus parvifolia	Chinese elm	5–9
Zelkova serrata	Sawleaf zelkova	5–9

*Varies with each species. See encyclopedia.

***Fagus sylvatica* 'Asplenifolia'**

***Thuja* species**

Trees that can be sheared

Few trees escape the pruning shears of the home gardener; pruning enhances structure and encourages healthy growth. Shearing, the indiscriminate cutting back of the entire tree canopy, is the simplest method of reducing the amount of foliage. Many trees respond poorly to this treatment. The following are some of the trees that can be sheared.

Botanical name	Common name	Zone
Cedrus species	Cedar	5–10*
Cupressocyparis leylandii		5–10
Cupressus species	Cypress	8–10
Ginkgo biloba	Maidenhair tree	5–10
Ilex species	Holly	6–10*
Laurus nobilis	Sweet bay	8–10
Ligustrum lucidum	Glossy privet	8–10
Malus species	Crabapple	2–9*
Olea europaea	Olive	9–10
Pittosporum species	Pittosporum	8–10*
Platanus acerifolia	London plane tree	5–9
Podocarpus macrophyllus	Yew pine	8–10
Pseudotsuga menziesii	Douglas fir	5–9
Thuja species	Arborvitae	3–9*
Tsuga canadensis	Canadian hemlock	4–8

*Varies with each species. See encyclopedia.

Trees with attractive fruits or berries

Bright colors aren't limited to foliage and flowers. Fruits and berries, both edible and inedible, can be just as attractive—and sometimes they last longer.

Botanical name	Common name	Zone
Amelanchier canadensis	Serviceberry	4–5
Arbutus species	Madrone	7–9
Chionanthus species	Fringe tree	5–8
Cornus species	Dogwood	5–9
Crataegus species	Hawthorn	4–9*
Diospyros species	Persimmon	5–9*
Elaeagnus angustifolia	Russian olive	1–8
Ilex species	Holly	6–10*
Koelreuteria paniculata	Goldenrain tree	5–9
Malus species	Crabapple	2–9*
Oxydendrum arboreum	Sourwood	6–9
Prunus species	Plums, cherries, cherry laurels	2–10*
Sorbus species	Mountain ash	2–7*

*Varies with each species. See encyclopedia.

***Ilex cornuta* 'Burfordii'**

Cornus florida 'Rubra'

Trees with color in more than one season

These trees provide interest over a long period of time with their flowers, fruits, autumn color, or bark.

Botanical name	Common name	Zone
Acer palmatum	Japanese maple	6–9
Amelanchier canadensis	Serviceberry	4–5
Betula species	Birch	2–10*
Cercis canadensis	Eastern redbud	2–8
Chionanthus virginicus	Fringe tree	5–8
Cladrastis kentuckea	Yellowwood	4–9
Cornus species	Dogwood	5–9
Crataegus species	Hawthorn	4–9*
Diospyros kaki	Kaki persimmon	7–9
Halesia carolina	Snowdrop tree	5–10
Ilex species	Holly	6–10*
Koelreuteria paniculata	Goldenrain tree	5–9
Lagerstroemia indica	Crape myrtle	8–10
Malus species	Crabapple	2–9*
Oxydendrum arboreum	Sourwood	6–9
Prunus species	Plums, cherries, cherry laurels	2–10*
Pyrus calleryana	Callery pear	5–9
Stewartia pseudocamellia	Japanese stewartia	8–9
Styrax japonicus	Japanese snowbell	5–9

*Varies with each species. See encyclopedia.

Dual-purpose trees

These are the ornamental edibles—trees that look decorative in the garden, and provide the added bonus of edible fruit.

Botanical name	Common name	Zone
Amelanchier canadensis	Serviceberry	4–5
Carya illinoinensis	Pecan	6–9
Diospyros species	Persimmon	5–9*
Eriobotrya japonica	Loquat	7–9
Malus species	Crabapple	2–9*
Olea europaea	Olive	9–10
Prunus species	Plums, cherries, cherry laurels	2–10*
Ziziphus jujuba	Chinese jujube	6–9

*Varies with each species. See encyclopedia.

Malus species

Wall trees

The trees on this list have well-behaved root systems and habits that allow for close planting to walls—ideal for softening the side of a one-to-two story building.

Botanical name	Common name	Zone
Acer species	Maple (columnar forms)	3–9*
Agonis flexuosa	Peppermint tree	9–10
Betula species	Birch	2–10*
Calocedrus decurrens	Incense cedar	5–10
Carpinus betulus 'Fastigiata'	European hornbeam	4–9
Chamaecyparis lawsoniana	Lawson cypress	6–9
Crataegus phaenopyrum	Washington thorn	5–9
Cryptomeria japonica	Japanese cedar	6–9
Eucalyptus species	Eucalyptus	9–10*
Ilex opaca	American holly	6–7
Laurus nobilis	Sweet bay	8–10
Malus species	Crabapple	2–9*
Maytenus boaria	Mayten tree	9–10
Picea glauca	White spruce	3–4
Podocarpus macrophyllus	Yew pine	8–10
Pyrus species	Pear	8–10*
Sequoia sempervirens	Coast redwood	7–10

*Varies with each species. See encyclopedia.

Malus species

Trees that tolerate seashore conditions

Use these trees as your first line of defense along the coast. Many will lose their natural habit of growth and become sculpted by the ocean winds.

Botanical name	Common name	Zone
Acer platanoides	Norway maple	4–9
Acer rubrum	Red maple	3–7
Arbutus species	Madrone	7–9
Carpinus betulus	European hornbeam	4–9
Cupressus macrocarpa	Monterey cypress	8–10
Elaeagnus angustifolia	Russian olive	1–8
Erythrina species	Coral tree	10
Eucalyptus species	Eucalyptus	9–10*
Hakea laurina	Sea urchin tree	10
Juniperus virginiana	Eastern red cedar	3–7
Leptospermum laevigatum	Tea tree	9–10
Metrosideros excelsus	New Zealand Christmas tree	10
Nyssa sylvatica	Black tupelo	5–9
Picea glauca	White spruce	3–4
Pinus species	Pine	3–9*
Platanus acerifolia	London plane tree	5–9
Populus nigra 'Italica'	Lombardy poplar	2–6
Salix alba vitellina	Golden willow	2–9
Ulmus parvifolia	Chinese elm	5–9

*Varies with each species. See encyclopedia.

Cupressus macrocarpa

Gleditsia triacanthos var. **inermis**

Trees that will stand abuse

You may call some of these trees "undesirables," but that won't stop them from growing where all else fails.

Botanical name	Common name	Zone
Acacia melanoxylon	Blackwood acacia	9–10
Carya illinoinensis	Pecan	6–9
Casuarina cunninghamiana	Beefwood	6–7
Celtis occidentalis	Common hackberry	5–8
Elaegnus angustifolia	Russian olive	1–8
Eucalyptus species	Eucalyptus	9–10*
Fraxinus species	Ash	3–9*
Ginkgo biloba	Maidenhair tree	5–10
Gleditsia triacanthos var. *inermis*	Thornless common honeylocust	5–9
Juniperus virginiana	Eastern red cedar	3–7
Malus species	Crabapple	2–9*
Melia azedarach	Chinaberry	7–10
Melia azedarach 'Umbraculifera'	Texas umbrella tree	7–10
Platanus acerifolia	London plane tree	5–9
Populus species	Poplar	2–10*
Rhus lancea	African sumac	8–10
Robinia pseudoacacia	Black locust	4–9
Salix species	Willow	2–9*
Ulmus species	Elm	3–9*

*Varies with each species. See encyclopedia.

Fraxinus pennsylvanica

Trees that stand flooding

Plant flood-tolerant trees in urban landscapes where soils may be excessively wet; such as low-lying, poorly drained areas. Shoreline plantings should also be adaptable to periodic flooding. The trees listed here can survive in standing water for 50 days or more.

Botanical name	Common name	Zone
Acer saccharinum	Silver maple	3–7
Betula nigra	River birch	5–10
Celtis occidentalis	Common hackberry	5–8
Diospyros virginiana	American persimmon	5–9
Fraxinus pennsylvanica	Green ash	3–8
Gleditsia triacanthos var. *inermis*	Thornless common honeylocust	5–9
Liquidambar styraciflua	American sweet gum	6–10
Nyssa sylvatica	Black tupelo	5–9
Platanus acerifolia	London plane tree	5–9
Populus species	Poplar	2–10*
Quercus phellos	Willow oak	6–9
Salix species	Willow	2–9
Taxodium distichum	Bald cypress	5–10

*Varies with each species. See encyclopedia.

Gleditsia triacanthos var. **inermis**

Liquidambar styraciflua

Trees that are essentially pest-free

Don't choose a tree just because it resists pests. And bear in mind that "pest-free" is a relative term, depending on locality. These trees are pest-free where well-adapted.

Botanical name	Common name	Zone
Cedrus species	Cedar	5–10*
Celtis species	Hackberry	6–9*
Cercidiphyllum japonicum	Katsura	4–9
Chionanthus virginicus	Fringe tree	5–8
Elaeagnus angustifolia	Russian olive	1–8
Eucalyptus species	Eucalyptus	9–10*
Ginkgo biloba	Maidenhair tree	10
Koelreuteria paniculata	Goldenrain tree	5–9
Laurus nobilis	Sweet bay	8–10
Liquidambar styraciflua	American sweet gum	6–10
Magnolia species	Magnolia	4–10*
Metasequoia glyptostroboides	Dawn redwood	6–10
Nyssa sylvatica	Black tupelo	5–9
Olea europaea	Olive	9–10
Ostrya virginiana	American hop hornbeam	4–9
Phellodendron amurense	Amur oak	4–9
Pistacia chinensis	Chinese pistachio	6–10
Sophora japonica	Japanese pagoda tree	5–10
Stewartia species	Stewartia	6–9*
Taxodium distichum	Bald cypress	5–10
Zelkova serrata	Sawleaf zelkova	5–9

*Varies with each species. See encyclopedia.

Pistacia chinensis

Magnolia soulangiana

Trees for fragrance

Although the flowers of some trees are inconspicuous, their presence in the garden is a decided olfactory pleasure. This list omits trees whose leaves are fragrant when crushed.

Botanical name	Common name	Zone
Acer ginnala	Amur maple	5–8
Cladrastis kentuckea	Yellowwood	4–9
Elaeagnus angustifolia	Russian olive	1–8
Halesia carolina	Snowdrop tree	5–10
Magnolia species	Magnolia	4–10*
Malus species	Crabapple	2–9*
Oxydendrum arboreum	Sourwood	6–9
Prunus species	Plums, cherries, cherry laurels	2–10*
Robinia pseudoacacia	Black locust	4–9
Sophora japonica	Japanese pagoda tree	5–10
Styrax japonicus	Japanese snowbell	5–9
Syringa reticulata	Japanese lilac tree	4–8
Tilia cordata	Littleleaf linden	4–9

*Varies with each species. See encyclopedia.

Populus species

Trees that look good in a grove

A grove is a group of trees in an open area. It is usually made up of one type of tree, which can be found in a pure stand somewhere in nature. If you have the space to plant one, a grove can provide pleasure when seen from a distance, as well as being a tranquil retreat.

Botanical name	Common name	Zone
Betula species	Birch	2–10*
Fagus sylvatica	European beech	5–10
Pinus species	Pine	3–10*
Populus species	Poplar	2–10*
Quercus species	Oak	4–9*
Tsuga species	Hemlock	4–8*

*Varies with each species. See encyclopedia.

Trees for screens and buffers

These trees are useful for hiding areas that are unattractive but necessary.

Botanical name	Common name	Zone
Abies species	Fir	4–8*
Acacia melanoxylon	Blackwood acacia	9–10
Acer campestre	Hedge maple	5–8
Calocedrus decurrens	Incense cedar	5–10
Cedrus deodara	Deodar cedar	7–10
Chamaecyparis obtusa	Hinoki false cypress	5–8
Cupressus species	Cypress	5–10*
Elaeagnus angustifolia	Russian olive	1–8
Eucalyptus species	Eucalyptus	9–10*
Ilex species	Holly	6–10*
Juniperus species	Juniper	3–10*
Laurus nobilis	Sweet bay	8–10
Ligustrum lucidum	Glossy privet	8–10
Olea europaea	Olive	9–10
Picea species	Spruce	3–9*
Pinus species	Pine	5–9*
Populus species	Poplar	2–10*
Prunus species	Plums, cherries, cherry laurels	2–10*
Sequoia sempervirens	Coast redwood	7–10
Thuja occidentalis	American arborvitae	3–9
Thuja plicata	Western red cedar	5–9
Tsuga canadensis	Canadian hemlock	4–8

*Varies with each species. See encyclopedia.

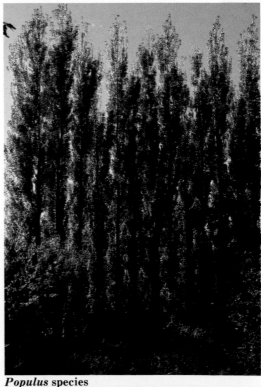
Populus species

Koelreuteria paniculata

Trees that stand city conditions

These trees vary in local adaptation, but all tolerate city conditions such as air pollution, reflected heat, and limited open soil surface for air and water.

Botanical name	Common name	Zone
Acacia melanoxylon	Blackwood acacia	9–10
Acer species	Maple	3–9*
Aesculus carnea	Red horsechestnut	4–8
Carpinus betulus	European hornbeam	4–9
Casuarina cunninghamiana	Beefwood	6–7
Catalpa species	Catalpa	5–10
Celtis occidentalis	Common hackberry	5–8
Chionanthus virginicus	Fringe tree	5–8
Cotinus coggygria	Smoke tree	5–9
Crataegus species	Hawthorn	4–9*
Eucalyptus species	Eucalyptus	9–10
Fraxinus species	Ash	3–9*
Ginkgo biloba	Maidenhair tree	5–10
Gleditsia triacanthos var. *inermis*	Thornless common honeylocust	5–9
Ilex opaca	American holly	6–7
Koelreuteria paniculata	Goldenrain tree	5–9
Laurus nobilis	Sweet bay	8–10
Malus species	Crabapple	2–9*
Nyssa sylvatica	Black tupelo	5–9
Ostrya virginiana	American hop hornbeam	4–9
Phellodendron amurense	Amur oak	4–9
Pinus nigra	Austrian pine	4–8
Pinus sylvestris	Scotch pine	3–8
Pistacia chinensis	Chinese pistachio	6–10
Platanus acerifolia	London plane tree	5–9
Pyrus calleryana	Callery pear	5–9
Quercus species	Oak	4–9*
Robinia pseudoacacia	Black locust	4–9
Sophora japonica	Japanese pagoda tree	5–10
Tilia cordata	Littleleaf linden	4–9
Ulmus species	Elm	3–9*
Zelkova serrata	Sawleaf zelkova	5–9

*Varies with each species. See encyclopedia.

Summer-flowering trees

Many trees are colorful long after the first spring blooms are over. Here are some summer-flowering trees.

Botanical name	Common name	Zone
Albizia julibrissin	Silk tree	7–10
Catalpa species	Catalpa	5–10
Chionanthus virginicus	Fringe tree	5–8
Cladrastis kentuckea	Yellowwood	4–9
Cornus kousa	Kousa dogwood	5–9
Cotinus coggygria	Smoke tree	5–9
Crataegus phaenopyrum	Washington thorn	5–9
Erythrina species	Coral tree	10
Franklinia alatamaha	Franklinia	6–8
Jacaranda acutifolia	Jacaranda	10
Koelreuteria paniculata	Goldenrain tree	5–9
Laburnum watereri 'Vossii'	Golden-chain tree	5–9
Lagerstroemia indica	Crape myrtle	8–10
Liriodendron tulipifera	Tulip tree	5–9
Magnolia grandiflora	Southern magnolia	7–9
Oxydendrum arboreum	Sourwood	6–9
Sophora japonica	Japanese pagoda tree	5–10
Stewartia species	Stewartia	6–9*
Styrax japonicus	Japanese snowbell	5–9
Syringa reticulata	Japanese lilac tree	4–8

*Varies with each species. See encyclopedia.

Liriodendron tulipifera

Indoor trees

Under greenhouse conditions, most trees can be grown indoors for a time. Here are a few outdoor trees suitable for common indoor conditions.

Botanical name	Common name
Araucaria heterophylla	Norfolk Island Pine
Cedrus species	Cedar
Chamaecyparis species	False cypress
Citrus species	Citrus
Grevillea robusta	Silk oak
Laurus nobilis	Sweet bay
Ligustrum lucidum	Glossy privet
Pittosporum species	Pittosporum
Podocarpus macrophyllus	Yew pine

Grevillea robusta

Small garden and patio trees

These are small, well-behaved trees that provide shade and seasonal show while allowing for patio and garden activities.

Botanical name	Common name	Zone
Acer species	Maple	3–9*
Amelanchier canadensis	Serviceberry	4–5
Bauhinia species	Orchid tree	7–10*
Cercidiphyllum japonicum	Katsura	4–9
Cercis canadensis	Eastern redbud	2–8
Chionanthus virginicus	Fringe tree	5–8
Cornus species	Dogwood	5–9
Cotinus coggygria	Smoke tree	5–9
Crataegus species	Hawthorn	4–9*
Eriobotrya japonica	Loquat	7–9
Halesia carolina	Snowdrop tree	5–10
Koelreuteria paniculata	Goldenrain tree	5–9
Lagerstroemia indica	Crape myrtle	8–10
Leptospermum laevigatum	Tea tree	9–10
Magnolia species	Magnolia	4–10*
Malus species	Crabapple	2–9*
Maytenus boaria	Mayten tree	9–10
Ostrya virginiana	American hop hornbeam	4–9
Oxydendrum arboreum	Sourwood	6–9
Pistachia chinensis	Chinese pistachio	6–10
Prunus species	Plums, cherries, cherry laurels	2–10*
Pyrus calleryana	Callery pear	5–9
Pyrus kawakamii	Evergreen pear	8–10
Sophora japonica	Japanese pagoda tree	5–10
Stewartia koreana	Korean stewartia	6–9
Styrax japonicus	Japanese snowbell	5–9
Syringa reticulata	Japanese lilac tree	4–8

*Varies with each species. See encyclopedia.

Prunus species

Cornus species

Pinus strobus

Betula maximowicziana

Prunus species

Trees with interesting bark

Texture, color, and patterns of bark are important considerations when selecting landscape trees.

Botanical name	Common name	Zone
Acer species	Maple	3–9*
Arbutus species	Madrone	7–9
Betula species	Birch	2–10*
Calocedrus decurrens	Incense cedar	5–10
Cladrastis lutea	Yellowwood	4–9
Cryptomeria japonica	Japanese cedar	6–9
Diospyros species	Persimmon	5–9*
Eucalyptus species	Eucalyptus	9–10*
Fagus sylvatica	European beech	5–10
Lagerstroemia indica	Crape myrtle	8–10
Liquidambar styraciflua	American sweet gum	6–10
Ostrya virginiana	American hop hornbeam	4–9
Pinus species	Pine	3–10*
Platanus acerifolia	London plane tree	5–9
Prunus species	Cherry	4–10*
Salix alba vitellina	Golden willow	2–9
Stewartia species	Stewartia	6–9*
Ulmus parvifolia	Chinese elm	5–9

*Varies with each species. See encyclopedia.

Lagerstroemia indica

Quercus agrifolia

Skyline trees

These are the stately giants that can be seen for blocks. They need lots of space to grow in and be appreciated

Botanical name	Common name	Zone
Acer species	Maple	3–9*
Carya illinoinensis	Pecan	6–9
Cedrus species	Cedar	5–10*
Cupressus sempervirens	Italian cypress	8–10
Eucalyptus species	Eucalyptus	9–10*
Fagus sylvatica	European beech	5–10
Ginkgo biloba	Maidenhair tree	5–10
Gleditsia triacanthos var. *inermis*	Thornless common honeylocust	5–9
Liquidambar styraciflua	American sweet gum	6–10
Liriodendron tulipifera	Tulip tree	5–9
Metasequoia glyptostroboides	Dawn redwood	6–10
Nyssa sylvatica	Black tupelo	5–9
Picea species	Spruce	3–9*
Pinus species	Pine	3–10*
Populus nigra 'Italica'	Lombardy poplar	2–6
Quercus species	Oak	4–9*
Sequoia sempervirens	Coast redwood	7–10
Taxodium distichum	Bald cypress	5–10
Tsuga canadensis	Canadian hemlock	4–8

*Varies with each species. See encyclopedia.

Trees with excellent fall color

In many parts of the country, trees offer a breathtaking kaleidoscope of fall color. Here are trees with reliable fall color.

Botanical name	Common name	Zone
Acer species	Maple	3–9*
Amelanchier canadensis	Serviceberry	4–5
Betula species	Birch	2–10*
Cercidiphyllum japonicum	Katsura	4–9
Cornus species	Dogwood	5–9*
Cotinus coggygria	Smoke tree	5–9
Diospyros virginiana	American common persimmon	5–9
Franklinia alatamaha	Franklinia	6–8
Fraxinus species	Ash	3–9*
Ginkgo biloba	Maidenhair tree	5–10
Lagerstroemia indica	Crape myrtle	8–10
Larix leptolepis	Japanese larch	5–8
Liquidambar styraciflua	American sweet gum	6–10
Liriodendron tulipifera	Tulip tree	5–9
Nyssa sylvatica	Black tupelo	5–9
Oxydendrum arboreum	Sourwood	6–9
Pistacia chinensis	Chinese pistachio	6–10
Populus species	Poplar	2–10*
Pyrus calleryana	Callery pear	5–9
Quercus species	Oak	4–9*
Sapium sebiferum	Chinese tallow tree	8–9
Sassafras albidum	Sassafras	5–9
Zelkova serrata	Sawleaf zelkova	5–9

*Varies with each species. See encyclopedia.

Acer species

Trees with attractive winter silhouette

When leafless, these trees provide a handsome outline against the open sky or a background of evergreens. They are winter's visual delights.

Botanical name	Common name	Zone
Acer species	Maple	3–9*
Alnus species	Alder	3–9*
Betula species	Birch	2–10*
Carpinus betulus	European hornbeam	4–9
Cercidiphyllum japonicum	Katsura	4–9
Cladrastis lutea	Yellowwood	4–9
Cornus florida	Flowering dogwood	5–9
Fagus sylvatica	European beech	5–10
Ginkgo biloba	Maidenhair tree	5–10
Gleditsia triacanthos var. *inermis*	Thornless common honeylocust	5–9
Ilex opaca	American holly	6–7
Lagerstroemia indica	Crape myrtle	8–10
Liquidambar styraciflua	American sweet gum	6–10
Liriodendron tulipifera	Tulip tree	5–9
Magnolia species	Magnolia	4–10*
Malus species	Crabapple	2–9*
Metasequoia glyptostroboides	Dawn redwood	6–10
Nyssa sylvatica	Black tupelo	5–9
Phellodendron amurense	Amur oak	4–9
Pistacia chinensis	Chinese pistachio	6–10
Platanus acerifolia	London plane tree	5–9
Populus species	Poplar	2–10*
Quercus species	Oak	4–9*
Salix species	Willow	2–9*
Stewartia koreana	Korean stewartia	6–9
Ulmus parvifolia	Chinese elm	5–9
Zelkova serrata	Sawleaf zelkova	5–9

*Varies with each species. See encyclopedia.

Salix matsudana

ENCYCLOPEDIA

Use this encyclopedia to find specific information on the trees you have chosen to fill your particular needs, or use it as a guide to identify existing trees and expand your knowledge about the trees in your landscape.

The following encyclopedia of trees does not begin to cover all the trees in the great world of trees. These trees were selected for their outstanding qualities, their availability, and their frequency in the landscape across the United States.

The trees are listed alphabetically by botanical name. The first entry for each genus is marked by a gray band. If you do not know the botanical name you can find it by looking up the common name in the index on pages 109–112.

The botanical name is given in the following way. The first word is the genus, always written in bold, with the first letter capitalized:

Gleditsia

This is followed by the species, which is also bold but not capitalized:

Gleditsia triacanthos

If there is a varietal name (the name for a plant that differs slightly from the species and occurs in the wild) it follows the genus and species and is written in bold after the abbreviation for the word variety (var.):

Gleditsia triacanthos var. inermis

Finally, the cultivars (the cultivated varieties) are capitalized and in single quotes:

Gleditsia triacanthos var. inermis 'Sunburst'

Hortus III is the reference used for the botanical nomenclature in this encyclopedia. If any of the entries are known by another name, it is in parenthesis below the first name.

The second unit of information is the common name, appearing in italics below the botanical name.

The next information given is whether the tree is evergreen, deciduous, or a needled evergreen; the zones in which it grows; the country or region of its origin; and finally its growth habit.

All these terms describing habit are, of course, relative:

Fast-growing, for example, may have different meanings in different locales. In this book fast-growing means an annual growth of more than 2 feet in height.

Moderate-growing, in relation to the definition of fast-growing, means growth of 1 to 2 feet in height per year.

Slow-growing, in relation to the terms used above, means a growth of less than one foot in height per year.

Height is also relative. It depends on soil, water, and other environmental factors. A Douglas fir that matures at 200 feet in an Oregon forest will attain only 20 feet at maturity in the Chisos Mountains of the Big Bend country of Texas. If the tree stands among other trees, it may have no other way to grow except up. We give the height the tree should reach in 50 or 60 years if it were standing alone.

In the fall, a quilt-like pattern is created on a hillside when evergreen trees are interspersed with autumn colored deciduous trees.

Left: The large green and orange flowers of the tulip tree, *Liriodendron tulipifera*, sit above the leaves but are not immediately noticeable. A careful eye will detect them among the surrounding foliage.

Abies concolor

Acacia baileyana

Acacia farnesiana

Abies species
Fir

The many species of fir available vary according to location. All form perfectly pyramidal trees that need a good deal of room to develop.

The fir is best used in open lawns, parks, or golf courses and grows well in moist, well-drained, nonalkaline soils, protected from high winds. It is a poor choice for hot, dry areas, but grows naturally in cold climate conifer forests where it may reach to 200 feet.

Abies concolor
White fir

Needled evergreen
Zones 4–8
Native to the western United States.
Moderate-growing to 80–100 feet; can grow to 200 feet.

The white fir is more tolerant of heat, drought, and city conditions than other fir species. The needles are blue-green or gray-green and about 2 inches long. Horizontal branches hold upright cylindrical cones that cluster on upper branches. Younger trees have smooth gray bark and make fragrant container Christmas trees.

Abies nordmanniana
Nordmann fir

Needled evergreen
Zones 5–8
Native to Asia Minor and the Mediterranean.
Slow- to moderate-growing to 55–65 feet.

Dark, shiny green needles with silver undersides densely cover the horizontal branches. Like *Abies concolor,* it can be grown in a container for several years and makes an excellent Christmas tree.

Abies procera
Noble fir

Needled evergreen
Zones 5–7
Native to the northwestern United States.
Fast-growing to 100–150 feet.

One of the most handsome of all firs, the noble fir forms a narrow tree with a stiff branching habit and blue-green foliage closely arranged on the twigs. It needs a cool climate in order to thrive.

Acacia species
Acacia

This large group of evergreen trees, with typically bright yellow flowers, is quite familiar to westerners.

Acacia baileyana
Bailey acacia, cootamunda wattle

Evergreen
Zones 9–10
Native to Australia.
Fast-growing to 20 feet tall and 20 feet wide.

The first flower color to announce the coming of spring, this acacia blooms at an early age with the daffodil-yellow flowers for which it is famous. A mature tree in full bloom is an unforgettable sight. The mass of bright color eclipses the foliage completely. *Acacia baileyana* with its fine, blue-gray ferny foliage is virtually foolproof but grows best in dry, well-drained soils.

Acacia baileyana 'Purpurea' is a beautiful variety with purple new growth.

Acacia farnesiana
Sweet acacia

Evergreen or deciduous depending on climate
Zones 9–10
Native to the southwestern United States and Mexico.
Fast-growing, wide-spreading, round-headed tree 12–15 feet high and 10–15 feet wide.

The breathtaking floral display appears any time from late fall to early spring, depending on the origin of the tree and the climate. Fragrant, pumpkin-yellow flowers bloom on delicate fernlike foliage.

This excellent specimen tree, patio tree, hedge, screen, or divider takes heat, drought, and alkaline soils. It is hardy to 16–18°F.

Acacia melanoxylon
Blackwood acacia

Evergreen
Zones 9–10
Native to Australia.
Fast-growing to 40 feet or more; upright with a broad pyramidal head.

This is a tree that will stand all types of abuse. The dark green leaves are 2–4 inches long and the flowers are inconspicuous. Use it as a fast-growing windbreak or screen, or as erosion control. The root system can break up pavement, so do not plant where this could be a problem.

Acacia pendula
Weeping myall

Evergreen
Zones 9–10
Native to eastern Australia. Fast-growing to 20–25 feet tall and about half as wide. Usually strong weeping form, occasionally dense and spreading.

A choice tree where a silvery-gray accent is required. It flowers sporadically in spring and attains a distinctive character with age.

Acer species
Maple

Variety in size, foliage and color is the key feature of the maples, both among and within the 90 species. The plant size ranges from 100-foot giants to low shrubs, while the leaves vary from broad 12-inch specimens to palmate ribbons 3 inches wide. White, yellow, many shades of green, pink, and maroon-red are found in the summer foliage, while the fall colors of yellow, orange, and red are legendary.

The constant features that help to identify maples are the winged seeds called samaras, and the opposite arrangement of the leaves and branches.

Verticillium wilt can be a problem, and so can aphids and the honeydew they secrete. A more irritating problem for a gardener is the fertility of some species and cultivars—especially as wind disperses the samaras or winged seeds over a wide area.

Acer buergeranum
Trident maple

Deciduous
Zones 7–9
Native to Japan and China. Grows to 50 feet with a narrow, rounded head.

The sharply three-pointed leaves explain the common name of this round-headed maple. It often grows with multiple stems and low branches, but it can be trained to a single stem and pruned for

head clearance. The 3-inch leaves are glossy green, turning yellow to red in the fall.

Acer campestre
Hedge maple

Deciduous
Zones 5–8
Native to Europe and Turkey. Slow to medium-growing to 25–40 feet tall and 20–25 feet wide.

This species is often trained as a hedge and is also useful as a small street tree. Although it grows best in well-drained soil, it will tolerate dry, poor, or sandy soils. The small 2- to 4-inch dull-green leaves turn yellowish in the fall.

Acer ginnala
Amur maple

Deciduous
Zones 5–8
Native to Siberia. Broad oval or globe shape; 20 feet tall and 20 feet wide.

This tree is both cold-tolerant and wind-tolerant and is usually a multiple-stemmed tree. Its fragrant flowers are a novelty among maples. Summer color is provided by the bright red fruit; later, the foliage also turns bright red. It is useful as a substitute for the Japanese maple in cold regions.

Acer oblongum
Evergreen maple

Evergreen
Zone 7
Native to China. Modest size of 20–25 feet in height with a weeping, almost pendulous form.

An anomaly among maples, this species is an evergreen where climates allow. The simple, elongated leaves are wholly unlike the traditional maple leaf. No special tricks are involved with its culture, but it's not for the cold maple climates; hardy only to 10 or 12°F. The milder the climate, the more evergreen the tree.

Acer palmatum
Japanese maple

Deciduous
Zones 6–9
Native to China and Japan. Slow-growing, small tree to 20 feet tall and 20 feet wide.

This is an extremely variable species that can even be

Acer campestre

Acer palmatum

Acer buergeranum

Acer campestre

Acer palmatum

Acer platanoides

Acer rubrum

Acer saccharum

Acer saccharinum

Acer rubrum

grown in a low mound. The 2- to 4-inch leaves, which have 5-inch lobes, can be almost round with small lobes or little more than leaf veins. Leaf color ranges from yellow-green to dark maroon-red in solid colors, and includes white and pink in variegated forms.

The color develops best in full sun but it may be necessary to grow this species in light shade if hot, dry winds are a problem. The following descriptions are of some of the selected forms.

'Atropurpureum' is one of the hardiest of the Japanese maples, with five-lobed leaves that remain red all summer.

'Osakazuki' has 7-lobed green leaves and bright red fall color.

'Dissectum' has finely divided cutleaf forms available with green or red leaves.

'Senkaki' is a green-leafed type with coral bark that is very attractive in the winter landscape.

Acer platanoides
Norway maple

Deciduous
Zones 4–9
Native to western Asia.
Grows 40–50 feet tall and 65–75 feet wide.

Over 20 selections of this variable, hardy species have been recorded. Many were selected for growth form, others for foliage color. The tree affords very dense shade and the yellow flowers produce a colorful display. The vigorous root system and dense shade made by the leaf canopy make it difficult to grow grass or other plants around the tree base. Some of the selected forms follow.

'Cleveland' is quite columnar as a young tree, eventually forming a broad oval, 50 feet tall and 25–30 feet wide. The dark green leaves are prone to leaf scorch in dry, hot weather. They turn yellow in fall.

'Crimson King' is probably the best-known variety of Norway maple. The leaves remain maroon-red throughout the season. Growth is somewhat slower than the green-leafed types, forming a tree 35–40 feet tall and 50 feet wide.

'Drummondii', with white-green leaves, gives a cool appearance on a hot day, al-though the white areas are apt to burn and the leaves often revert to the green form. It will form a tree 40–50 feet tall and 35–45 feet wide.

'Emerald Queen' is a fast-growing selection with an up-right, spreading form. It can be expected to grow 50 feet tall and 50 feet wide. It is one of the best cultivars for yellow fall colors.

'Globe' is a very dense, spreading form. The ultimate height is determined by grafting height. When grafted at 6–7 feet, it will grow 20–25 feet tall and 35–45 feet wide. It is more susceptible to aphids than other cultivars.

'Summer Shade' is a fast-growing selection that should grow to 45–50 feet with a 60–70 feet spread. The heavy-textured leaves are more heat-tolerant than most of the species.

Acer rubrum
Red maple, swamp maple

Deciduous
Zones 3–7
Native to southern and mid-western United States.
Fast-growing to a height of 50–60 feet tall and 40–60 feet wide; symmetrical, spreading, pyramidal.

This is a fast-growing species with relatively small leaves and strong wood. It does not produce shade as dense as the other large maples. The common names indicate two features of this species: its attractive, small red flowers in early spring, and its ability to grow in wet as well as normal soil; developing fall color under both conditions.

Many selections have been made for growth form and fall color.

'Autumn Flame' forms a round-headed tree, 30–40 feet tall and wide. This selection consistently colors orange-red 1–2 weeks before the others. Leaf fall is also 1–2 weeks earlier. In areas of short growing seasons, fall colors occur before killing frost.

'Bowhall' is a narrow, pyramidal form 45 feet tall and 15 feet wide and develops good fall color. It is useful near buildings and streets where other trees with wider spreading limbs could be hazardous.

'Scanlon' has the same char-

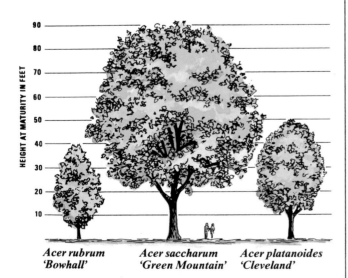

Acer rubrum   *Acer saccharum*   *Acer platanoides*
'Bowhall'   'Green Mountain'   'Cleveland'

HEIGHT AT MATURITY IN FEET

acteristics and appears to be identical to 'Bowhall.'

'Red Sunset' is also a broad, pyramidal tree, 50–60 feet tall and 30–40 feet wide. Heavy production of red flowers in spring and midseason and red fall foliage make this one of the most colorful selections.

Acer saccharinum
Silver maple, soft maple

Deciduous
Zones 3–7
Native to the flood plains of the midwestern, northeastern, and southern United States.
Fast-growing to 100 feet with a broad, open crown 70 feet wide; no fall color.

Heat and dry winds have less of an adverse effect than on other maples, so it is used for quick shade where other trees fail. Limb breakage in wind or storms is a serious problem with this species. Because of this, some cities have prohibited planting the silver maple as a street tree. Check local ordinances before planting this tree on the street.

Acer saccharum
Sugar maple, rock maple

Deciduous
Zones 3–7
Native to the midwestern, northeastern, and southern United States.
Forms a majestic tree 80–100 feet tall and 60–80 feet wide when grown in the open.

This maple supplies much of the fall color in New England when it turns from yellow to orange and finally to red. It is also the source of syrup for maple syrup and the lumber for maple furniture. It is a hardy tree but does not grow well in inner city or hot, dry conditions. It is more susceptible to damage done by soil compaction and paving than most maples.

The following are the best selections of this species.

'Newton Sentry' develops a central leader, and a narrow, columnar form.

'Temple's Upright' does not have a central leader but does maintain a columnar form.

'Green Mountain' has the typical broad, oval shape of the species, but the dark green leaves are resistant to adverse conditions.

Acrocarpus fraxinifolius
Pink cedar

Deciduous
Zones 8–10
Native to India.
Fast-growing to anywhere from 30–60 feet; sometimes taller in favorable conditions.

The common name of this fall tree is pink Indian cedar, but it should not be confused with other cedars because it is definitely not coniferous. *Acrocarpus* has large, intricately compound leaves dispersed at the branch terminals in a manner that makes for an open, lacy canopy throughout the warm months, and a pleasing though bare structure for a brief period in winter. Flowers are small and not showy but new growth, produced at intervals throughout spring and summer, is a delightful rosy-bronze that imparts to this species a distinction rarely found in shade trees.

Aesculus carnea
Red horsechestnut

Deciduous
Zones 4–8
A hybrid of *Aesculus hippo-castanum* (native to southern Europe) and *Aesculus pavia* (native to the southeastern United States).
Slow to moderate-growing to 30–50 feet tall and 30 feet wide. Pyramidal when young, erect with round crown when mature.

This spectacular flowering tree is at its best in midspring when it bears upright 8- to 10-inch-long, red to pink flower spikes. Five-fingered leaves are light to dark bright green and tropical looking. A very manageable garden, street, or park tree that casts dense shade. Because it is subject to leaf scorch in hot dry winds, this tree is best in cool, moist summer areas and protected locations.

'Briotii' is a cultivar that has bright red flowers in clusters up to 9 inches long.

Agonis flexuosa
*Peppermint tree,
Australian willow myrtle*

Evergreen
Zones 9–10
Native to southwestern Australia.

Acer saccharinum

Acer saccharum

Aesculus x carnea 'Briotii'

Albizia julibrissin

Alnus rhombifolia

Amelanchier canadensis

Moderate- to fast-growing rate to 25–30 feet tall and at least as wide; weeping branches in spreading, irregular horizontal pattern.

This excellent, small evergreen tree derives its name from the smell of the crushed leaves. The pliable wood, drooping branches, and long, thin, willow-like leaves make this an attractive, light, and airy tree. White flowers bloom in early summer, new growth is tinged coppery red, and the interesting bark sheds with age.

A good lawn, patio, or tub tree that is drought tolerant, heat tolerant, pest-free, and can be espaliered.

Albizia julibrissin
Silk tree, mimosa

Deciduous
Zones 7–10
Native to Asia from Iran through Japan.
Fast-growing to 25–40 feet and greater in width; arching branches form a beautiful umbrellalike canopy, sometimes twice as wide as tall; most useful when multitrunked.

This tree is beautiful in summer when the showy pink powder-puff-like flowers are held above the fernlike, almost feathery, light green leaves. The light-sensitive foliage folds at night.

The silk tree can be anything from a street tree to a ground cover depending on how it's pruned; but because of the many flowers and its relatively short life it is not the best possible choice for a street tree. It is good in a lawn and can be planted in a container just as long as it gets plenty of heat and an alkaline soil. Flowers are most attractive if seen from above.

'Rosea' has rich pink flowers and is the hardiest form.

'Charlotte' and 'Tryon' are both wilt resistant. This is quite important in the Northeast and South and especially the Midwest, where wilt can be a big problem.

Besides wilt, other problems are weak wood and twig girdlers. Prune widespreading branches to help relieve weight that could cause them to break off from the tree.

Alnus cordata
Italian alder

Deciduous
Hardy to zone 5
Native to Corsica and southern Italy.
Grows to 40–70 feet; pyramidal in habit.

This is the least moisture-demanding and best behaved alder. Valued in the warm southwest.

Alnus glutinosa
Common alder, black alder, European alder

Deciduous
Hardy to zone 3
Native to western North America.
Fast-growing to 40–60 feet tall and 20–40 feet wide.

This is a valuable tree for wet areas in the East. It will even grow under water and it does well in poor soils.

Alnus rhombifolia
White alder

Deciduous
Zone 4
Native to the northwestern United States and Canada.
Fast-growing to 60–70 feet tall and about two thirds as wide; upright irregular form, gracefully pendulous branch tips.

This tree is most valuable for a quick screen in poorly drained soils. Leaves are dark green above, paler beneath. The catkins give a purple haze to a grove of white alder as winter ends.

Alnus rubra
(A. oregona)
Red alder

Deciduous
Hardy to zone 4
Native to western North America.
Fast-growing to 40–70 feet with a slender, pyramidal habit.

This 'weed' tree of the Pacific coastal areas has some points of considerable merit. It will invade nearly any area denuded of cover, since it has the same capabilities as do members of the pea family to host nitrogen-fixed bacteria in its roots. It will thrive in low, damp soil situations and grows rapidly enough to be a commercial source of firewood. As a temporary shelter wood for more permanent and more attractive trees and shrubs, it is unsurpassed.

Amelanchier canadensis
Serviceberry, shadblow, shadbush, juneberry

Deciduous
Zones 4–5
Native to Canada and to the northern and midwestern United States.
Moderate growth to 20–40 feet; often multistemmed with an upright, twiggy form.

Serviceberry is one of the earliest trees to flower in the East. The snow-white blossoms appear just after the flowers of the cornelian cherries and dogwoods, but before eastern redbud. This durable all-season perfomer displays beautiful autumn color.

Araucaria araucana
Monkey-puzzle tree

Needled evergreen
Zones 9–10
Native to Chile.
Slow- to moderate-growing to 60–70 feet tall and 30–35 feet wide; erect, pyramidal with branches in regular whorls.

This is more of an oddity than an effective landscape tree. Dark green, stiff, and sharp, the large needles arm the upward sweeping branches giving them a tubular look, often thought to be exotic. The name comes from the fact that once a monkey climbs up this tree, it can't climb down again.

This tree needs room to develop and the lower branches often die out. A well-drained soil with plenty of water is important.

Araucaria bidwillii
Bunya-bunya

Needled evergreen
Zones 9–10
Native to Australia.
Moderate-growing to 30–50 feet tall and 35–55 feet wide; dense pyramidal, round top, broader with age.

The bunya bunya can be grown in a container as a small indoor tree, but it will reach up to 50 feet when grown outdoors.

The overlapping leaves are dark green, sharp, and stiff, and the unusual branches curve with upsweeping tips.

Araucaria heterophylla
Norfolk Island Pine

Needled evergreen
Zones 9–10
Native to Norfolk Island (1,000 miles east of Australia).
Moderate-growing to 60–70 feet tall and half as wide. Formal pyramid with symmetrical branching in horizontal tiers.

This tree has a softly formal character and grows quite large in the landscape. It grows well near the coast.
During Victorian times this tree was most widely known as a container tree. It was recently reintroduced as an indoor plant.

Arbutus menziesii
Madrone, madrona

Evergreen
Zones 7–9
Native to the Pacific Northwest and southern California.
Slow- to moderate-growing to as high as 80 feet in native stands; usually smaller, to 20–40 feet, with a broad, irregular round head.

This is a tree with color in all seasons. The new foliage is soft and light green to copper in color. Older leaves become leathery and dark green above with gray undersides. It is especially attractive in groves and grows well near the coast.

Arbutus unedo
Strawberry tree

Evergreen
Zones 7–9
Native to the Mediterranean countries and Ireland.
Slow- to moderate-growing to 10–25 feet tall and equally wide; irregular rounding habit.

A handsome, shrubby plant that needs pruning to make a well-formed tree. Suckers grow readily and must be cut back. Leaves are dark green with red stems. Small white, urn-shaped flowers are followed by fruit that look like strawberries but taste like cotton.
The twisting, almost bonsai-like habit of the tree becomes more attractive with age. The bark is smooth, deep-red to brownish red.
The tree is best used where it can be looked up into, such as on the patio or lawn. It is widely adaptable to soil and climate.

Bauhinia species

These stunning flowering trees are common to southern California and Florida. All *Bauhinias* like a warm, well-drained spot, but suffer in high heat and drought. They are excellent small shade trees and flower best with applications of a low nitrogen fertilizer.

Bauhinia blakeana
Hong Kong orchid tree

Deciduous
Zones 9–10
Native to Southeast Asia.
Moderate-growing rate to 20 feet; flat-topped, unbrellalike canopy.

The Hong Kong orchid tree loses most of its kidney-shaped leaves just long enough to display beautiful pink to purple, orchidlike flowers in late fall to early winter. The flowers are up to 5 to 6 inches wide, which is larger than on most *Bauhinias*.

Bauhinia forficata
Brazilian orchid tree

Deciduous
Zones 9–10
Native to Brazil.
Moderate-growing to 15–20 feet; umbrellalike canopy.

The creamy white flowers appear in spring. Hardiest of the *Bauhinias*, this tree has dark green foliage that grows on interesting twisted branches.

Bauhinia variegata
Orchid tree

Deciduous
Zones 7–10
Native to India and China.
Moderate-growing rate to 20–25 feet with umbrellalike form; tends to get bushy and multitrunked.

This is the *Bauhinia* most common to southern California. It is quite variable in flower and foliage color depending on soil conditions, climate and exposure. A mild, dry winter produces the most spectacular bloom. The most common flower shades are from white to pink to lavender. Its leaves are gone briefly dur-

Araucaria heterophylla

Arbutus menziesii

Arbutus unedo

Bauhinia blakeana

Betula pendula

Betula nigra

Betula papyrifera

ing flowering. This is an excellent street tree in the right climate. Select grafted varieties for consistent flower color.

'Candida' has white flowers.

Deciduous
Zones 6–10
Native to Japan.
Fast-growing to 80–100 feet with a wide spreading, rounded crown.

This tree has the largest leaves and catkins of all birches. The older bark is white while the younger branches are reddish brown. The older, white bark splits and hangs from the tree in shreddy clumps. This large tree must be planted where it has enough room to develop.

Monarch birch is tolerant of both cold, windy areas and dry sites as long as it has good drainage.

Betula nigra
River birch

Deciduous
Zones 5–10
Native to the eastern, midwestern and southern United States.
Grows 50–70 feet at maturity; pyramidal in habit.

This is the birch of the South and the most widely adapted. It is native along river banks and on flood plains. The young bark is red, gradually becoming an attractive, shaggy, chocolate brown with age.

Roots of river birch must reach moist soil to thrive. This is a good tree to use as a drought indicator, as it is the first to show moisture stress.

Betula papyrifera
Paper birch

Deciduous
Zones 3–8
Native to areas from eastern Canada to Alaska.
Grows to 40–60 feet at maturity; open and erect habit.

In the north country, the birch is often called "the lady of the forest." Its white bark brings a lively grace to a group of needled evergreens, and in the winter its white bark and blue-gray branches provide a cheerful and colorful contrast to the typical dark brown of other leafless trees. The peeling bark was used by Indians to make canoes.

In general, white birches are trees of the north. Borer injury is a limiting factor unless they are grown in cold areas.

The natural habit of the birch is to grow in clumps of several trees. Clump planting is suggested as a variation on the typical spacing of 6 feet.

Betula pendula
European white birch

Deciduous
Zones 2–10
Native to Europe and Asia Minor.
Grows to about 60 feet.

Rough, warty twigs and white bark with vertical black markings distinguish this birch from others. Older trees often have pendulous branches. Borer injury can become a serious problem on this birch.

The following are common cultivars:

'Fastigiata,' the pyramidal European white birch is columnar and dense when young: As it matures, it developes its pyramidal shape.

'Gracilis,' the cutleaf European white birch has finely dissected leaves.

'Tristis,' the slender European white birch, is a tall, graceful tree with slender pendulous branches.

The messiest pests of birches are the honeydew-dripping aphids. Another pest, the bronze birch borer, can be damaging, particularly to older birches. It is best to grow birches in areas with cold winter climates where this borer is not such a problem.

The birch leafminer can be very damaging, particularly to older birches. Gray, paper, and European white birches are most susceptible. Damage that shows up as blotches or blisters on newly developing leaves is caused by the larvae of the black sawfly as they feed between the two surfaces of the leaf. Look for them about the time the leaves are half open. There are later (but less damaging) generations, the second one appearing at the end of June. The insecticides dimethoate or Orthene® can control these pests.

Brachychiton species

These evergreen or deciduous flowering trees thrive in warm inland areas. Three completely different trees fall under this label.

Brachychiton acerifolius
Flame tree

Deciduous
Zones 9–10
Native to Australia.
Fast-growing to 55–60 feet or more; upright, pyramidal form.

This tree produces incredible amounts of small, almost tubular, scarlet to orange flowers in late spring and early summer. In a good year the tree may be completely covered with blossoms. Large shiny green leaves with 5 to 7 lobes and 10 inches across drop just before the tree flowers. Ornamental fruits are boatlike in appearance and the trunk of the tree is green. Withhold water in spring for best flowering.

Brachychiton discolor
Queensland lacebark, scrub bottle tree

Deciduous
Zones 9–10
Native to Australia.
Moderate-growing to 40–90 feet; hardy to 25 feet; narrow pyramidal in youth, wider with age.

Another fine tree for warm inland areas. The six-inch, somewhat maple-like leaves are woolly white beneath and dark green above. They fall just before the flowers appear. Following sudden cold weather, the entire tree may be bare for a period. Blossoms of rose to pink are backed by short brown wool, which also distinguishes the six-inch rusty seed pods. This tree is especially handsome for avenue planting where there is ample sun and heat.

Brachychiton populneus
Kurrajong

Evergreen
Zones 9–10
Native to Australia.
Slow- to moderate-growing to 25–50 feet; dense conical crown.

The heavy, tapering trunk resembles a bottle and the foliage is similar to that of poplars. The leaves may vary on the same tree from lobed to nonlobed. Small, white bell-shaped flowers are followed by canoe-shaped seed pods. These are attractive in dried arrangements but create some litter under the tree.

The tree is extremely useful in hot areas because it is drought resistant and is also effective as a screen or windbreak.

Callistemon citrinus
Lemon bottlebrush

Evergreen
Zones 8–10
Native to Australia.
Fast-growing to 20–25 feet; narrowish round-headed.

Lemon bottlebrush has year-round flower color and pinkish-copper new leaves that contribute to its appeal. It is amazingly tolerant of both heat and cold. A suitable screen or buffer that can be used espaliered or as a single-trunked specimen.

Calocedrus decurrens
Incense cedar

Needled evergreen
Zones 5–10
Native to the mountains of southern Oregon, California, western Nevada, and Baja California.
Slow-growing in youth, but becomes fast-growing, reaching 70–90 feet; dense pyramidal form.

The common name best describes this tree's most familiar feature. The rich green foliage is aromatic and most apparent in hot weather. The attractive reddish-brown bark is usually concealed by the foliage. This is a handsome tree if given space and is quite useful as a tall hedge and windbreak.

Carpinus betulus
European hornbeam

Deciduous
Zones 4–9
Native to Europe and Asia Minor.
Slow- to moderate-growing to 30–40 feet tall and 10–15 feet wide; dense pyramidal shape.

Carpinus betulus

Betula pendula 'Gracilis'

Catalpa bignonioides **Casuarina cunninghamiana**

Catalpa speciosa

Cedrus atlantica 'Glauca'

This is a neat, manageable, attractive tree with dark green, elmlike foliage and smooth gray bark that becomes beautifully fluted with old age. Fall color is yellow and the dark leaves remain until spring. The interesting fruit clusters are nutlike in appearance.

'Fastigiata' is the most available and trouble-free variety. This tree consistently scores in the top five at the Shade Tree Evaluation Plot in Wooster, Ohio. One of the best choices for hedges and screens, it is also an excellent street tree and effective wall tree. It is tolerant of air pollution and soils that range from dry and rocky to wet but well-drained.

Other varieties available are 'Pyramidalis' and 'Columnaris.'

Carya illinoinensis
Pecan

Deciduous
Zones 6–9
Native to the southeastern United States.
Moderate-growing to 100 feet and equally wide with a rounded crown.

No tree in the southern landscape contributes more as a shade tree and as a food tree. It has held its place in the affection of home gardeners in spite of its susceptibility to diseases—most notably scab.

There is much interest in the introduction of the pecan into the warm interiors of California. Many varieties are being tested. Ask your County Extension office for a listing.

In the alkaline soils of arid Arizona and New Mexico, pecans should be sprayed for zinc deficiency. Check with your local County Extension Agent.

Casuarina cunninghamiana
Beefwood, river she-oak

Evergreen
Zones 6–7
Native to Queensland and New South Wales.
Fast-growing to 70 feet; pine-like with spreading drooping branches.

Beefwood is a rugged tree, valuable for quick effects. It does well in the Pacific south-

west, the Gulf coast and in Florida. The long, thin branches have leaves that look like needles. The fruit is woody, grayish, and conelike. This is the most graceful of the casuarinas.

Catalpa bignonioides
Common southern catalpa, Indian bean, cigar tree

Deciduous
Zones 5–10
Native to the southeastern United States.
Fast-growing to 35–40 feet and nearly as wide; irregular, broad, rounded crown.

When grown in full sun, this tree is covered with white, trumpet-shaped flowers in late spring to early summer. The flowers are spotted with yellow, purple, and brown. The blooms are followed by long, 13- to 18-inch bean pods which last into winter and can be a nuisance in a lawn. The name Indian bean or cigar tree came from the fact that Indians once smoked the pods of this tree.

Common catalpa is widely adapted to soils and climates, stands city smog, and is best used in large areas, like parks, to accent bold features. This is a messy tree, constantly dropping pods, blossoms, leaves, and twigs. It can be drastically pollarded.

Catalpa speciosa
Northern catalpa, western catalpa

Deciduous
Zones 5–10
Native to the eastern United States.
Fast-growing to 65–75 feet; round-headed.

Very similar to *C. bignonioides,* northern catalpa has larger leaves, fewer flowers, and is slightly hardier. It is also larger and should be used only in areas that allow it plenty of space.

Cedrus atlantica
Atlas cedar

Needled evergreen
Zones 7–10
Native to the Middle East and North Africa.
Slow- to moderate-growing to 40–60 feet tall and 30–40 feet wide; irregular pyramidal

when young; wide pyramidal to open, with broadly spreading crown, at maturity.

The fine-textured, bluish-green needles are borne in stiff clusters. The picturesque growth habit becomes most spectacular with room and time to mature. A fine skyline tree that is moderately drought resistant, unsuitable for small city lots, but excellent in parks, large gardens, or planted along a boulevard. It is the most popular of the blue-foliaged conifers wherever it can be grown. The cultivar 'Glauca' has the richest blue-colored foliage.

Cedrus deodara
Deodar cedar

Needled evergreen
Zones 7–10
Native to the Himalayas.
Fast-growing to 40–75 feet tall and 20–45 feet wide.

This is the most refined, graceful and soft textured cedar. Lower branches sweep to the ground while upper branches are evenly spaced and well pronounced. The foliage grows in typical cedar clusters but is a soft light green color. This is the fastest growing of the cedars.

The nodding tip of this tree makes it very recognizable on the skyline. It may be used as a screen, but there are better choices. Good as a wall tree when there is space in front; good in parks and in groves. Like other cedars, it needs space to be appreciated but responds to pruning for confinement.

Cedrus libani
Cedar of Lebanon

Needled evergreen
Zones 6–10
Native to Asia Minor.
Grows to 40–70 feet with a large, thick trunk and wide-spreading branches.

This true cedar has bright green foliage but is very similar to *Cedrus atlantica*. It is slower growing and hardier.

Celtis species
Hackberry

Hackberries are known for their persistence in tough situations. They stand drought, hot, dry winds, city conditions, and are relatively pest-free.

Celtis australis
European hackberry

Deciduous
Zones 7–9
Native to Southern Europe.
Moderate-growing to 40–70 feet tall and 40–50 feet wide.

Celtis australis has dark green leaves with finely toothed edges. The small, edible, dark purple berries it bears are prized by birds. This is a great tree for tough, arid regions: Use as a shade tree, in the lawn, or even as a street tree.

Celtis laevigata
Sugar hackberry, Mississippi hackberry

Deciduous
Zones 6–9
Native to the south central and southeastern United States.
Slow- to moderate-growing to 30–50 feet tall and slightly less wide.

An upright, spreading tree with dark green foliage that shows little color change in the fall. The bark of the trunk and the larger branches is gray, like that of the American beech. The sugar hackberry is tolerant of a wide range of soil conditions and is less susceptible to 'witch's broom' than the common hackberry.

Celtis occidentalis
Common hackberry

Deciduous
Zones 5–8
Native to the central and southeastern United States.
Moderate-growing to 35–45 feet tall and equally wide; irregular to round-headed; spreading, sometimes pendulous branches.

The common hackberry has bright green leaves with finely toothed edges and dark red berries that attract birds. Its one drawback is "witch's broom," a foliage and branch deformation. There appear to be great possibilities for selection of resistant cultivars, as exhibited by the recent introduction 'Prairie Pride.'

This is a valuable shade tree in tough situations and has been used in shelter belts in the Great Plains.

Cedrus deodara

Cedrus libani

Celtis occidentalis

Cercidiphyllum japonicum

Cercis canadensis

Chamaecyparis lawsoniana

Ceratonia siliqua
Carob, St. John's bread

Evergreen
Zones 9–10
Native to eastern Mediterranean countries.
Moderate-growing to 25–40 feet and equally as wide; naturally shrubby but easily trained into a round-headed tree.

The dense, dark green head of this tree casts deep shade. The leaves are divided into 4 to 10 leaflets. Flowers are not ornamental and are foul-smelling on male trees. The flowers are followed by long, twisting, dark brown seed pods on female trees. The large, brown pods can be a nuisance when they drop in the garden or on the street.

Effective as a shrubby hedge or screen, the carob tree takes well to shearing, and is widely adapted. It grows wherever the olive tree will and takes heat and drought as well as city conditions.

The pods of the carob tree are ground into powder and used as a substitute for chocolate.

Cercidiphyllum japonicum
Katsura

Deciduous
Zones 4–9
Native to Japan.
Slow-growing to 40 feet tall or greater and slightly less wide.

Trained as a single-trunked tree, it is upright and narrow, but will become spreading and vase-shaped with age. It is broad and spreading, branching upward and outward if left multitrunked. An excellent tree for filtered shade. Some trees are naturally single-stemmed and are segregated as the variety 'Sinense.'

The leaves are a lustrous reddish to reddish-purple in spring when they first unfold. In the summer, foliage is dark green, neat and crisp, and later turns scarlet and gold in the fall. Small, dry fruit capsules provide winter ornamentation. Katsura is pest-free and tolerant of moist soil and shade but must be protected from hot sun and drying winds.

Cercis canadensis
Eastern redbud

Deciduous
Zones 5–8
Native to southeastern Canada and the eastern United States.
Moderate-growing to 25–35 feet tall and equally wide; irregular round head with attractive horizontally tiered branches.

Eastern redbud is best known for its magenta-colored pea-shaped flowers that bloom on bare branches in spring, a few weeks before dogwood. Blossoms form right on the trunk of this tree. This all-seasons performer has attractive green heart-shaped leaves, yellow fall color, and interesting seed pods. In winter, the lovely reddish-brown bark shows off the zig-zag structure of the branches.

You can grow eastern redbud under almost any conditions; sun, shade, acid soil, alkaline soil, and moist soils. The only problem you will run into with this tolerant and beautiful tree is that it is susceptible both to wilt and to borers.

Chamaecyparis species
False cypress

Out of this large group of plants, the following are useful as wall trees, lawn specimens, and especially screens or tall hedges; good tub trees when young. They are adapted to cool, coastal conditions, but can take moist heat; protect from hot, dry winds. Fake cypress is best grown in moist, well-drained soil. This tree is most widely known in its dwarf forms.

Chamaecyparis lawsoniana
Lawson cypress, Port Orford cedar

Needled evergreen
Zones 6–9
Native to southwestern Oregon and northwestern California.
Fast-growing to 60–70 feet tall and one-third as wide; pyramidal with wide-spreading, pendulous branches.

This very graceful tree has branches that end in lacy sprays of bright green to blue-green. Scalelike leaves, nodding tip, and soft brown to reddish-brown fibrous bark are its distinguishing features.

Many varieties are available, varying in form and foliage color. This tree is subject to cypress root rot in the Northwest: Check with your County Extension Agent's office for rot resistant plants.

Chamaecyparis nootkatensis
Alaska cedar

Needled evergreen
Zones 5–9
Native to Alaska, British Columbia, and northern Oregon.
Moderate-growing to 70–100 feet; narrow, columnar habit with strong, irregular branching and pendulous branch tips.

The dark green foliage of this tree has a characteristic and strong fragrance when crushed. Alaska cedar tolerates poor soil conditions but needs full sun and thrives in a moist, well-drained, acid soil. It is native to harsh climates and tolerates low temperatures. This is a beautiful and durable landscape tree.

Chamaecyparis obtusa
Hinoki false cypress

Needled evergreen
Zones 5–8
Native to Japan
Slow-growing to 40–50 feet tall and 15–25 feet wide; pyramidal.

The foliage is deep, shiny green in thick, horizontally flattened sprays. Branch tips are slightly pendulous, but not so distinctly as Lawson cypress.

Many varieties, including useful dwarf forms, are usually more readily available than the species. The following are some of the favorites.

'Crippsii' has golden new growth, which reaches a height of 30 feet.

'Gracilis,' with its very dark, shiny green foliage and somewhat weeping form, grows to 20 feet by 4–5 feet.

'Nana Gracilis' is very dwarf. It was recorded to have grown only 9 feet in 66 years at the Secrest Arboretum in Wooster, Ohio.

Chamaecyparis pisifera
Sawara false cypress

Needled evergreen
Zones 4–8
Native to Japan
Moderate-growing to 20–30 feet tall and half as wide; pyramidal.

This tree is less dense than *Chamaecyparis obtusa.* The loosely arranged, scalelike leaves of the species are bright, glossy green Lower branches are lost early in life, revealing reddish-brown bark that peels in long strips. Inner branches often die out; encourage new growth with annual pruning.

Chionanthus virginicus
Fringe tree

Deciduous
Zones 5–8
Native to southeastern United States.
Slow-growing to 20–30 feet with a round crown wider than tall.

The foliage of the fringe tree is heavy textured and bold, almost suggesting a magnolia; it turns yellow in autumn. Foliage and flowers show late in the spring, well after danger of frost has passed.

A dependable late spring bloomer with white threadlike petals that form delicate fleecy clusters. The white pendulous blooms are certainly among the most delicate and refined of any woody plant. They are aromatic and persist into early summer. Pendulous clusters of dark blue berries on female trees are a lasting feature in the fall.

A good tree for a small property, the fringe tree works especially well near a patio. Deep-rooted and multi-trunked (almost more of a shrub than a tree), it requires special shaping or training if a tree form is desired.

Cinnamomum camphora
Camphor tree

Evergreen
Zones 6–12
Native to China and Japan.
Slow-growing to 50 feet tall or greater with wider spread; round-headed, with limbs spreading upward.

Deservedly popular as a resi-

dential and street tree in the Southwest and South, the camphor tree creates dense shade. Attractive, aromatic, shiny yellow-green foliage contrasts with the reddish new leaves. Yellow flower clusters are fragrant, although not showy. The camphor tree makes a good street tree if given room but does poorly in heavy alkaline soils.

Cladrastis Kentuckea
Yellowwood

Deciduous
Zones 4–9
Native to North Carolina and Kentucky.
Moderate-growing to 30–35 feet tall and 20–25 feet wide. Upright, with spreading branches forming a vase-shaped crown.

Yellowwood has attractive, smooth, beechlike gray bark and clean foliage that turns clear yellow in the fall. Its crowning glory, however, is the wonderful June show of pure white, intensely fragrant flowers, pea-shaped and borne in clusters like white wisteria. Heavy flowering tends to occur in alternate years, and in a good year it's show is a wonderful experience.

The brown pods and zigzagging branches are of winter interest. A good lawn, patio, or park tree, although it is slow-growing and won't bloom until its 10 years old.

When mature, yellowwood withstands prolonged drought, heat, and extreme cold and tolerates alkaline, and wet soils.

Cornus species
Dogwood

The dogwoods include plants that range in size from the 6- to 9-inch bunchberry of the northern woodlands to the Pacific dogwoods, which may grow 70 feet or more in height. In general, dogwoods require a slightly acid soil with moderate moisture and good fertility, and they will grow well in full sun, except in hot climates where they must be partially shaded.

Dogwoods are well known for their beautiful foliage and flowers. Many have the added attraction of interesting bark and fruits.

Chamaecyparis pisifera

Chionanthus virginicus

Cladrastis lutea

Cornus alternifolia

Cornus florida 'Rubra'

Cornus florida var. *rubra*

Cotinus coggygria

Cornus alternifolia
Pagoda dogwood

Deciduous
Zones 5–9
Native to North America,
Europe, and Asia.
Grows to 15–25 feet tall and
equally wide.

Pagoda dogwood is less showy
than other species, but it is
hardier and is useful in the
harsh climate of the midwestern states and adjacent
southern portions of Canada.
The branches are arranged in
distinct, flat tiers, and like
many other dogwoods, the
white flowers are attractive,
and the fall color is good.
There is a variety with white
variegation, but the leaves
burn badly in summer heat.

Cornus florida
Flowering dogwood

Deciduous
Zones 5–9
Native to the eastern United
States.
Moderate-growing, rarely ex-
ceeding 30 feet; variable habit
from pyramidal to umbrella to
wide-spreading and flat.

The flowering dogwood is a
tree with many seasons of
interest. The display of
flowers in the spring is won-
derfully showy. In the fall, the
leaves turn a rich brocade of
red and crimson. The berries,
borne in clusters, are a rich,
glossy red, and often persist
after the leaves have fallen.
Even in winter, the layered
"oriental" branching habit and
the myriads of conspicuous
flattened flower buds are
decorative. This particular
dogwood is susceptible to
fungal wilt disorders and to
borer problems.

The following are some of the
outstanding varieties available.

'Cherokee Chief' is a relatively new, deep pink flowering dogwood from Tennessee.
It has a much deeper, richer
color than the older *C. florida*
var. *Rubra,* but it is not as
winter hardy as the old original
pink dogwood that comes from
Pennsylvania.

'Cloud Nine,' an extremely
profuse white bloomer from
Alabama, is noted for the many
large flowers borne on even a
young tree. It is slow-growing,
and smaller than most of the
other varieties at maturity,
which makes it a fine choice for
planting wherever space is
limited. It is of southern origin
and not hardy in areas with
cold winters (zone 4).

'New Hampshire,' one of the
hardiest of all the selections of
Cornus florida, this tree
blooms regularly each year in
southern Vermont and New
Hampshire where it origi-
nated. It "burns up" in the hot
southern summers, but it
grows well and blooms profusely throughout zone 4.

Cornus florida 'Rubra'
Of the many pink forms, this
one with especially rich color
was discovered early, propagated, and named the red
flowering dogwood. Its color
varies somewhat depending on
the soil in which it is grown and
the age of the flowers, but
newly opened flowers are a
deep, full pink. It is most
admired when planted in combination with white-flowering
specimens.

Cornus kousa
*Kousa dogwood, Japanese
dogwood*

Deciduous
Zones 5–9
Native to Japan and Korea.
Slow- to moderate-growing to
15–20 feet, spreading; tends
to be multi-trunked.

A dual-purpose tree with fruits
that are favored by birds and
by some people. Like the
serviceberry, it is another
3-season small tree: it flowers
a month after *Cornus florida.*
For October and November
fruits appear that are rasp-
berrylike but larger. This is a
beautiful tree that should be
grown on a single stem.

Cotinus coggygria
Smoke tree

Deciduous
Zones 5–9
Native to southern Europe and
central China.
Moderate- to fast-growing to
15–25 feet tall and equally
wide; broad urn-shape with
rounded top.

This is actually a shrub, but a
little pruning can produce an
attractive, multitrunked tree
form. Although it blooms at
the beginning of summer, the
feathery masses of fine grey or
purplish hairs give the tree a
smokelike appearance as they

fade. These last throughout the entire summer. Normal leaf color is blue-green.

It is a good patio tree, and can also be planted in groups. Widely adaptable, this tree prefers good drainage and blooms best in infertile, dry soils. It is drought-tolerant and easy to grow.

Crataegus species
Hawthorn

The hawthorns, the toughest of our flowering trees, form a group of quite similar, thorny, small trees. With very few exceptions, they all bear white flowers, have showy red or orange fruits, and thrive even in adverse situations—in the inner city, along highways, and at the seashore where salt spray is a hazard to most trees. The only drawback is their susceptibility to fire-blight. They bloom in late May after most of the spectacular spring-flowering trees have faded. Many species have fine glossy foliage and the fruits of most are exceptionally long lasting.

Crataegus x lavallei
Lavalle hawthorn

Deciduous
Zones 5–9
Cross between *Crataegus crus-galli* and *Crataegus pubescens*
Moderate-growing to 20 feet with a dense, oval head.

The white flowers are large and abundant and the foliage is glossy green in summer and bronze-red in the fall. The orange to red fruits last well into the winter.

Crataegus monogyna
'Stricta'
Singleseed hawthorn

Deciduous
Zones 5–9
Native to England and Europe. Grows to 20–30 feet tall and 8–9 feet wide with upright branches and a narrow habit.

A singleseed hawthorn that is used as a hedge plant and as an understock for the grafted varieties of hawthorn. This variety is one of the best narrow trees for urban situations. It is almost completely thornless, and bears white flowers in small clusters in late May.

Crataegus oxyacantha (C. laevigata)
English hawthorn

Deciduous
Zones 5–9
Native to England and Europe. Moderate-growing to 15–25 feet high and equally wide; shrublike and round-headed with low branching.

This is the other abundant European species, the most common country hedge plant throughout England. It is also the most variable of all the hawthorns; single and double-flowered trees have been found with white, pink, and red flowers. Unfortunately, the species does poorly in summer heat and humidity. The leaves, being subject to fungus diseases, drop off to leave the twigs bare during most of the summer months. The following are some of the best varieties.

'Alba Plena' is a 15 foot tall, wide-spreading tree bearing myriads of double pure white flowers in late May. The flowers are sterile but they last a long time, gradually turning a pale pink. This particular cultivar bears very little fruit, but holds its foliage quite well in the East.

'Autumn Glory' is noted for its very large and long-lasting red fruits. This one grows very rapidly and reaches 18 feet in height at maturity and bears single white flowers in May.

'Crimson Cloud,' a recent introduction, is the best of the hawthorns with colored flowers for eastern conditions. It bears clouds of bright crimson flowers, each with a white star in the center to give it sparkle. The foliage is leathery, fine textured, and highly resistant to leaf spot disease. It grows into a tall, oval tree 20 feet in height, and thrives under city conditions. The fruits on this cultivar are glossy red and they remain on the tree well into the winter.

'Paulii,' Paul's scarlet hawthorn, is certainly one of the most beautiful varieties wherever the climate suits it. The flowers are fully double and an intense rosy-red color, but they are not followed by fruit. It develops into a full, rounded tree.

Crataegus x lavallei

Crataegus oxycantha

Crataegus phaenopyrum

Crataegus oxycantha 'Autumn Glory'

Crataegus phaenopyrum

Crataegus viridis 'Winter King'

Cryptomeria japonica

Cupressocyparis leylandii

Crataegus phaenopyrum
Washington thorn

Deciduous
Zones 5–9
Native to the southern United
  States.
Grows 20–30 feet tall and
  20–25 feet wide; broad,
  columnar, and dense with
  thorns.

The splendid, glossy foliage
turns a beautiful orange-red in
the fall. This is the best of all
the hawthorns for fall color.
The flowers are abundant and
pure white, giving rise to large
clusters of scarlet fruit, which
are among the longest lasting
of all the species. It is quite
narrow and upright when
young, broadening with age.
Washington thorn is resistant
to fireblight and grows exceptionally well in the city—there
are specimens many decades
old that are still thriving in
mini-parks in downtown New
York City.

Crataegus punctata
Dotted hawthorn

Deciduous
Zones 5–9
Native to the United States
  and Canada.
Grows to 30 feet and has stout
  branches that are often
  thorny.

This is a hardy native species
with attractive silvery bark
and abundant fruit. It is one of
the few species that contains
individuals bearing yellow as
well as red fruits.
'Ohio Pioneer' is valued because it is virtually thornless,
making it useful for garden or
street planting.

Crataegus 'Toba'

Deciduous
Zones 4–9
Cross between *Crataegus
  succulenta* and *Crataegus
  oxycantha* 'Paulii.'
Grows to 15–20 feet.

This hardy and beautiful variety originated in the harsh
climate of Manitoba, Canada.
The flowers are borne abundantly every year and are a
pure white when they first
open, gradually deepening to a
rose color. They are fully
double and the tree fruits
rather sparsely. The leathery
foliage is a fine, dark green
color, immune to leaf spot dis-

eases and lasting throughout
the summer. It is almost
thornless and hence a most
useful flowering garden tree,
especially in cold areas where
most of the showy flowering
cherries and crabapples are
not hardy.

Crataegus viridis
'Winter King'

Deciduous
Zones 5–9
Native to the southern United
  States.
Grows to 35 feet with a
  rounded, dense head.

This tree has distinct green
stems with a waxy bloom and
fine glossy leaves. Its principal
merit is the production of
abundant and long-lasting red
fruits, making the leafless
trees a distinct patch of red in
the winter landscape. It has
vase-shaped branches when
young, forming a full rounded
head when mature.

Cryptomeria japonica
Japanese cedar

Needled evergreen
Zones 6–9
Native to Japan and China.
Moderate-growing to 70–90
  feet tall and half as wide;
  pyramidal, open form;
  rounded top with age.

The small, light green to
bluish-green needles and
drooping branches combine to
give this tree a soft, graceful
look. The needles pick up a
bronze tinge in winter and the
reddish-brown bark peels in
strips.
  This tree needs room to develop, eventually reaching
skyline status. A good park
tree, it likes ample water and a
well-drained deep soil but does
not like arid climates. It is relatively pest-free.
  'Elegans,' the plume cedar,
has soft, feathery foliage that
turns coppery-bronze in winter. It is slow-growing to a
20–25 foot dense pyramid.
Many cultivars, including
dwarf forms, are available.

Cupressocyparis leylandii

Needled evergreen
Zones 6–10
Cross of *Chamaecyparis
  nootkatensis* and *Cupressus
  macrocarpa*.

Fast-growing to 40–50 feet; columnar, loosely pyramidal with age.

This is one of the best fast-growing columnar plants for tall hedges and screens. Growth rate reports range from 3–5 feet a year, but sometimes it topples due to fast growth. The branching pattern is graceful, spreading in horizontal fans of gray-green to pale-green foliage. This tree is dense when young. It tolerates a wide range of soils and climates.

Cupressus glabra
Smooth Arizona cypress

Needled evergreen
Zones 7–10
Native to central Arizona.
Fast-growing to 35 feet tall and half as wide; compact, narrow pyramidal, becoming more open with age.

This cypress stands hot, dry desert conditions, and poor sandy soil. The straight trunk has reddish bark that eventually becomes brown and furrowed with age. The scale-like foliage is silver gray to blue-green. Smooth Arizona cypress is a good windbreak, screen, or hedge. Wet soil encourages shallow roots, which weakens the wind resistance.

Several selected forms with predictable shape and foliage color are available.

Cupressus macrocarpa
Monterey cypress

Needled evergreen
Zones 8–10
Native to the Monterey Peninsula in California.
Slow- to moderate-growing to 40–70 feet; narrow pyramidal; rounded with age.

This is the tree most associated with the California coastline. The windswept artistic habit develops properly only in high winds near the coast, and even then only with age. Young trees are symmetrical. This tree should not be grown far from the West Coast. It is valuable as a windbreak or clipped hedge, but subject to fatal canker disease. Ask your Country Extension Agent for information about the prevention and control of this disease.

Cupressus sempervirens
Italian cypress

Evergreen
Zones 8–10
Native to southern Europe and western Asia.
Fast-growing to 30–40 feet tall and 3–6 feet wide in strict vertical column.

Italian cypress is a dominant vertical element in any landscape, but must be used with caution. It is too stiff and formal for anything but a large garden or driveway approach. Many people use them thinking they will stay small, and they soon get out of scale.

This cypress tolerates a wide range of soils and drought, but not poor drainage. Scale-like, dull green leaves are borne on horizontal branches.

Several cultivars are more available than the species. Most have tighter habits and vary in foliage color from bright green to blue.

Diospyros kaki
Kaki persimmon, Japanese persimmon

Deciduous
Zones 7–9
Native to China and Korea.
Moderate-growing to 20–30 feet with a similar spread; low round head.

The new foliage is soft, light green, gradually turning a heavier dark green in the summer, and different shades of yellow, red, and orange before dropping in the fall. This is followed by bright orange fruits that light up the bare branches like Christmas tree ornaments; the bark is also attractive. The fruits, excellent both dried or fresh, are very sweet. Choice fruiting varieties include 'Chocolate', 'Fuyu', and 'Hachiya', which is also the most valuable as an ornamental tree.

A fine small garden shade tree. Its hardiness can be stretched by planting in portable containers, or as an espalier against a south wall. Few pests bother this tree. Constant moisture and early spring fertilizing will help reduce fruit drop.

Diospyros virginiana
American common persimmon

Cupressus sempervirens

Diospyros virginiana

Diospyros virginiana

Elaegnus angustifolia

Eriobotrya japonica

Erythrina caffra

Deciduous
Zones 5–9
Native to eastern United States.
Moderate-growing to 30–50 feet tall and half as wide; oval form.

American persimmon is hardier than the Oriental persimmon. Fruits ripen after the first frost, turning from astringent to sweet. This tree doesn't have the striking show of fruit on bare branches, but does provide the same interesting winter branch silhouette that the Oriental persimmon provides. The tree is easily identified by the small, uniform boxes deeply cut into the bark.

More widely adapted than the Oriental persimmon, the American persimmon tolerates a wide range of soils and climates. Male and female trees are required for fruit production.

Elaeagnus angustifolia
Russian olive

Deciduous
Zones 2–8
Native to Europe and western Asia.
Fast-growing to 20–25 feet and equally wide; shrubby, round-headed.

This is a good, tough tree; a problem solver in very cold or hot, dry areas. The leaves are willowlike, olive green above and silvery beneath. The usually crooked, twisted trunk has attractive shedding, dark-brown bark. The branches are thorny. Greenish-yellow flowers appear in early summer followed by quantities of yellow berries that furnish winter food for many kinds of birds.

Russian olive is widely adapted to all but poorly drained soils. Verticillium wilt can be a serious problem on this tree. The fruits are messy, making this a good tree to view from a distance. An excellent hedge or screen, it takes well to clipping even as an espalier. A good tree for erosion control or slope cover.

Eriobotrya japonica
Loquat

Evergreen
Zones 7–9
Native to China and Japan.
Moderate-growing to 30 feet and equally wide; broad, round, crownless.

A very ornamental, dual-purpose tree, with edible fruit. The most striking feature is the very large leaf, 6–12 inches long by 2–4 inches wide; prominently veined and serrated, dark green above with a downy rust-colored underside. The fragrant but small white flowers in the fall are followed by abundant orange to yellow fruits that ripen in late winter or early spring. The fruit has a large seed and is puckery if picked green but has a delicious flavor when ripe.

Amenable to pruning, the loquat can even be trained as a ground cover, and may be used as a landscape specimen, espalier, or in a container.

This mild-climate tree tolerates alkaline soil but needs good drainage, and is sometimes subject to fireblight.

The seedlings have unpredictable fruit quality but the cultivars are reliable. 'Gold Nugget' and 'Champagne' produce good fruit.

Erythrina species
Coral tree

These trees for mild climates bear spectacular conelike clusters of pea-shaped, orange-to-red flowers. The flower color does vary, so be sure to select from known cultivars. Growth is spreading and irregular, resulting in a bold and twisted habit as unique and identifiable as the olive. The branches are thorny and the leaves are divided into 3 leaflets. Climate adaptation varies according to species, but all demand moist, well-drained, rich soils, and full sun. They are only briefly deciduous.

Erythrina caffra
Kaffirboom coral tree

Deciduous
Zone 10
Native to South Africa.
Fast-growing to as high as 40 feet, but usually smaller; spreads wider than tall, with flattened crown.

The kaffirboom has large, wide-open scarlet blossoms. The dark green leaves drop prior to flowering in January then reappear in March. This is the best *Erythrina* for the coast.

Erythrina humeana
Natal coral tree

Deciduous
Zone 10
Native to South Africa.
Fast-growing to 25 feet, good garden size, spreading, most useful when multitrunked.

The bright orange-red flowers are held well above the dark green foliage. Blooms appear primarily in fall; in a warm sheltered location, the bloom period may be extended. Flowers begin at a young age.

Eucalyptus species
Eucalyptus

Of the nearly six hundred species of eucalyptus native to Australia, perhaps one hundred and fifty have been tested. Though most proved adaptable, surprisingly few are to be found in the local nursery trade. Eucalyptus are fast growing, essentially foolproof and maintenance-free. They require a mild climate. The litter of leaves and seed pods can be a problem, but nothing quite compares with their form— tall, graceful, evergreen, and responsive to the slightest breeze. This family has a vitality totally lacking in most other trees of comparable stature.

Because of their exceedingly rapid growth, eucalyptus trees should be set out at the smallest practicable size and given as little staking as possible.

All *Eucalyptus* species are deciduous and are native to Australia.

Eucalyptus camaldulensis
Murray River red gum

Evergreen
Zones 9–10
Native to Australia.
Rapid-growing to 75 feet with upright, spreading crown and pendulous foliage of long narrow leaves.

This is one of the very best of the big eucalyptus if there is plenty of planting space. It has an attractive mottled trunk, branches that intermittently shed stringy bark, and often rough, corky bark at the base. In extreme and most attractive cases, the slender branches hang straight down

for ten to fifteen feet. When established, this species takes either desert heat or heavy rainfall.

Eucalyptus cinerea
Florist's eucalyptus

Evergreen
Zones 9–10
Native to Australia.
Moderate- to rapid-growing to 30–40 feet.

In many respects, this is the best of the blue-gray group. A stronger grower than its look-alikes, *E. cinerea* has perfoliate (like shish-kebab) leaves in its juvenile stage that are used by florists either alone or with cut flowers. A good percentage of these leaves are retained as the long, narrow, mature leaves develop. The rough brown bark always retains the distinctive ashen tone that inspired the species name, *cinerea*. It tends to have multiple trunks but can be pruned to one. This tree remains garden size for at least the first ten years, and is a striking subject for the first five.

Eucalyptus cladocalyx
Sugar gum

Evergreen
Zone 10
Native to Australia.
Rapid-growing comparable to *E. camaldulensis* in scale, but not as hardy.

Sugar gum has a strong, upright form with interesting bark patterns and foliage concentrated at branch terminals. The scaffolding structure is essentially clear of leaves, which gives the effect of myriad leafy parasols on the crown. Sugar gum is especially good on the coast and does not need much water.

Eucalyptus ficifolia
*Flaming gum,
red-flowering gum*

Evergreen
Zone 10
Native to Australia.
Rapid-growing to 25 feet.

This tree enjoys coastal conditions that are much like those of its native land. Flaming gum is not a large tree as *eucalyptus* go, but it is a good specimen in full bloom with its bright red flowers. It has few equals for color. The leaves

Eucalyptus cladocalyx

Eucalyptus ficifolia

Eucalyptus ficifolia

Eucalyptus gunnii

Eucalyptus polyanthemos

Fagus sylvatica 'Pendula'

Fagus sylvatica

are dark green, large and heavy, which accounts for the name *ficifolia,* meaning "like a *ficus."* In form, this gum is chunky, with foliage so thick branches are all but hidden. It lacks the grace usually associated with the genus, but puts all its relatives to shame when in bloom. Coastal zones are best, as this one is on the frost-tender list.

Eucalyptus gunnii
Cider gum

Evergreen
Zone 9
Native to Australia.
Fast-growing to 50 feet;
  upright.

The hardiest tree in our list, this one has been known to accept temperatures down to 0° F. when established. A strong grower with the typical long, narrow, medium green leaves, *E. gunnii* is dense and sturdy enough to make a good windbreak. Its best use is in those districts too cold for other species.

Eucalyptus polyanthemos
Silver dollar eucalyptus

Evergreen
Zones 9–10
Native to Australia.
Fast-growing to 40–50 feet.

The silvery gray, juvenile leaves are rounded and suspended individually on light twigs. This is a good tough tree at home on the sea coast or in the desert, where it grows quite rapidly. As a young tree, the gray-green foliage is most attractive, but *E. polyanthemos,* lacking the inherent grace of *E. camaldulensis,* loses some of its charm with age.

Eucalyptus robusta
Swamp mahogany

Evergreen
Zones 9–10
Native to Australia.
Grows to 75 feet; heavy,
  upright structure.

This tree is well named both in the botanical and in the vernacular. It is robust in every sense and, though it will accept a Spartan existence, can comfortably tolerate as much as 100 inches of annual irrigation. *E. robusta* is too big for the garden, but is well-suited to a golf course or campus. The extra-large, thick leaves depart from the normal eucalyptus shape and are several shades greener. It's rough, corky bark is reddish-brown. The ivory-white flowers of *E. robusta* are more conspicuous than most *Eucalyptus* blossoms but are not very special.

Although hardy to 15°–20°F. when mature, it is a bit tender when young. Although swamp mahogany is a tempting windbreak, its heavy foliage and upright branches make it subject to breakage in strong winds.

Eucalyptus rudis
Desert gum

Evergreen
Zones 9–10
Native to Australia.
Fast-growing to 40–50 feet.

Desert gum is aptly named. *E. rudis* thrives on the extremes of southern California's Imperial Valley, and grows well in intense heat, strong wind, or poor soil. Once well-established, it needs little food or water. The bark is rough and dark brown at the base and very gray above. The foliage, rounded when young, matures to the typical long, narrow shape, quite gray in desert heat, but greener on the coast, where it also does very well.

Eucalyptus sideroxylon
Red ironbark

Evergreen
Zone 10
Native to Australia.
Moderate-growing to 40–50
  feet; narrowly upright.

Red ironbark is normally one of the big growers, but there are many natural variations in size as well as in color of leaf and flower. It is a fairly common tree on old city streets, parks, or golf courses, with grey-green foliage, often pendulous, and sometimes with very attractive rosy-red flowers. The ironbark is particularly tough, but not as rapid in growth as the other big types. As in the case of *E. ficifolia,* some clues to the mature trees can be perceived in nursery selection; darker leaves usually denote better flowers.

Eucalyptus viminalis
Manna gum

Evergreen
Zones 9–10
Native to Australia.
Fast-growing to 100 feet or
  more with sturdy, upreaching
  branches.

Though hard to imagine, it is surprising how many blue gums and manna gums were planted in modest parkways and gardens in Los Angeles during the early years of this century. Needless to say, anything short of a highway, golf course, campus, or a site of equal scale is going to be too tight a fit for this gum. It has clean, almost white bark, and rich green weeping foliage.

Eugenia uniflora
Surinam cherry, pitanga

Evergreen
Zone 10
Native to South America.
Moderate-growing to 13–25
  feet; dense and compact.

The glossy green leaves of Surinam cherry have a coppery tinge that darkens in cold weather. Mildly fragrant, brushlike, white flowers appear in late summer. The fruits turn from green to yellow to orange, and finally are bright crimson when edible. When they drop they can be quite messy and they sprout readily. Surinam cherry appreciates moist, well-drained soil. It may be damaged in cold years in zone 9, but it grows back. This tree is frequently and most effectively used as a tall hedge; more compact and attractive with shearing. This is one of the trees resistant to oak root fungus.

Fagus sylvatica
European beech

Deciduous
Zones 5–10
Native to central and southern
  Europe.
Slow-growing to 70–80 feet
  tall and 60 feet wide; dense
  pyramidal form.

European beech is prized for its smooth gray bark and glossy, dark green foliage, which takes on excellent fall color. The edible nuts attract wildlife.
  The bark of an old venerable

beech can be compared to the hide of an elephant. Some parts are smooth, while other parts look like wrinkled skin. The beech, like the huge elephant, needs and demands lots of room. Beeches are usually found growing in groves, and the sight of a beech grove is truly a sight to remember. The silvery gray bark brings a brightness to the area, even on a cloudy day, To do the beech full justice, it should be allowed to sweep the ground with its lower branches—which means a circular area of 50 to 60 feet, and often up to 90 feet. This makes it suitable for parks, golf courses, and a college campus, rather than the home garden.

'Asplenifolia', fernleaf beech, has refined, fernlike foliage, as the common name suggests.

'Pendula', weeping European beech, is one of the best weeping trees. Clean, dark green foliage grows on graceful pendant branches that sweep the ground.

'Riversii', River's purple beech, is considered to be the most beautiful of all purple-foliage trees. It resists drought and tolerates moist soil conditions.

Franklinia alatamaha
Franklinia

Deciduous
Zones 6–8
Native to Georgia.
Slow- to moderate-growing to 20–25 feet; upright, open pyramid.

Much has been written about the search for this tree. Once thought extinct, it was discovered growing in Georgia in the eighteen hundreds and has not been found in the wild since, although many have looked. It can, however, be found in cultivation and is well worth growing. Its beautiful, white camellialike flowers are often found on the tree at the same time the leaves are turning brilliant orange-red in the fall. The foliage is glossy green.

This tree is somewhat of a challenge to grow and has been known to die suddenly; but it is worth the effort. It prefers rich, acid soil, partial shade, and protection from wind. An unusual lawn or patio tree.

Fraxinus species
Ash

This large and versatile group of trees can fill almost any demand. One glaring weakness of the ash is its heavy seed production and the resulting seedlings, but this is being eliminated among the wide variety of seedless cultivars now available.

The ash's greatest beauty is found in its leaves. With a few exceptions, they are 6–12 inches long and divided into as many as 12–13 leaflets that can each be several inches long. They combine to form a beautiful, softly textured canopy casting a shade light enough to allow grass and other plants to grow beneath. The ashes are great as lawn trees or for any area needing lots of leafy shade.

Although there are many ashes commonly available, a few stand out as the most valuable and versatile.

Fraxinus excelsior
European ash

Deciduous
Zones 4–9
Native to Europe and Asia Minor.
Grows to 30–50 feet with a round head.

The single, glossy, dark green, leathery leaves distinguish this cultivar from other ashes. Although it doesn't show fall color, the leaves stay green late, contrasting nicely with brightly colored trees around it.

Variety 'Jaspidea' has golden bark and the leaves show fall color.

Fraxinus ornus
Flowering ash

Deciduous
Zones 6–8
Native to southern Europe and western Asia.
Grows to 35 feet with a round head.

The flowering ash is untypical of most ashes and best for cool areas. This ash bears fluffy white to greenish-white clusters of fragrant flowers in late spring. Shiny green leaves turn soft lavender or yellow in fall. The seed clusters are unattractive and remain on the tree well into winter.

Franklinia alatamaha

Fraxinus excelsior 'Jaspidea'

Fraxinus ornus

Ginkgo biloba

Gleditsia triacanthos
var. *inermis* 'Sunburst'

Gleditsia triacanthos
var. *inermis* 'Majestic'

Fraxinus oxycarpa
'Flame'
Claret ash

Deciduous
Zones 6–9
Native to southern Europe and western Asia.
Grows to a height of 30–40 feet; round-headed.

This tree has small, glossy, dark green leaves that turn wine-red in fall. The spreading habit and light shade make it a good selection for the yard.

Fraxinus pennsylvanica (F. lanceolata)
Green ash, red ash

Deciduous
Zones 3–8
Native to Nova Scotia, and to Georgia and Mississippi.
Moderate-growing to 30–50 feet; narrowly upright when young, growing into a compact, rounded habit.

The many attributes of this ash have brought about its widespread popularity. It will withstand wet soil, severe cold, and is also drought resistant. This vigorous tree is easy to grow.

Fraxinus velutina
'Modesto'
Velvet ash

Deciduous
Native to Arizona and New Mexico.
Grows to 50 feet with upright branching.

Though it has weak wood and is prone to anthracnose and mistletoe problems, the velvet ash is popular in mild climates because of its bright yellow fall color.

Ginkgo biloba
Maidenhair tree

Deciduous
Zones 5–10
Native to China.
Slow-growing to 60–100 feet, growth rate varies with climate. Specimens have grown 10 feet in 9 years at North Willamette Experiment Station in Aurora, Oregon. Conical and sparsely branched in youth; spreading and dense with age.

The maidenhair tree is one of the oldest living trees; fossil records of the genus date back 200 million years. The picturesque, irregular habit of growth is quite interesting, as are the bright green, fan-shaped leaves. They turn brilliant yellow in fall and drop all at once—sometimes overnight—a plus for those who don't like to rake often.

A remarkably tough tree that stands smoke and air pollution and ranks as one of the top ten trees for wide streets. It is pest-free and widely adaptable, demanding only a well-drained soil. It needs room to develop, and is excellent as a park or large lawn tree.

Because it is slow to respond after transplanting, the maidenhair tree will need extra watering. The seeds are highly valued in China and Japan, where they are roasted and eaten. They are supposed to aid digestion and "diminish the effects of wine." Male trees are preferred since berries of the female tree have a rancid odor when crushed.

Gleditsia triacanthos var. inermis
Thornless common honeylocust

Deciduous
Zones 5–9
Native to the eastern and central United States.
Moderate- to fast-growing to 30–80 feet tall and equally wide.

The honey locust leaf is delicate and compound with tiny leaflets, allowing filtered sunlight through. The lacy appearance gives the tree an almost tropical look, a rarity itself among trees hardy enough to live in the northern U.S.

Besides its light shade, the honeylocust has one other characteristic that favors good lawn growth. Turf is usually most vigorous in the cooler, moister seasons—early spring and late fall. By good fortune, the growth of the honeylocust favors lawn development by leafing out late in the spring and dropping its golden leaflets early in the fall. The leaflets require a minimum of raking.

Occasionally, new growth on young trees needs some pruning in midsummer to avoid an overgrown or weeping appearance. About one-half of the new growth should be cut off to allow new growth with stronger branches and a better shape to develop.

Honeylocust is tolerant of various environmental stresses, including air pollution and highway salting, and it is also quite resistant to wind damage. The upright branching habit, especially of young trees, allows them to survive much ice storm damage resulting from ice build-up on the twigs.

With all its advantages, the honeylocust does have some problems: the warmer the climate, the greater the problems. In certain southern localities mimosa webworm, pod gall, and plant bugs can be troublesome, so check locally to determine if these insects are prevalent in your area. Wilt has become a serious problem along the East Coast. This is a classic example of overplanting a pest-free tree and increasing the population until an otherwise unimportant pest gets completely out of control. Older trees, whose vigor is reduced because of age or site, should be pruned quite severely once every 2–4 years.

The following are some of the cultivars that have been developed.

'Imperial' has a moderate growth rate to 35 feet. The round crown is symmetrical and spreading. The bright green foliage casts heavy shade because of the closely spaced leaves and dense branching.

'Majestic' is compact with a fast growth rate to 45–55 feet. This tree is not as dense as 'Skyline' or 'Imperial.' It has a spreading crown and dark green foliage.

'Moraine' is the first cultivar to be patented. It is fast-growing and vase-shaped, to 40–50 feet. The trunk may be curved when young, requiring more training if a straight trunk is desired.

'Ruby Lace,' with its fast-growing, spreading habit, reaches 30–35 feet. The new foliage is purplish-bronze, maturing to green. Because this tree is of controversial beauty, try to see an older one before buying. It may need extra pruning in youth.

'Shademaster' is a fast grower to 40–50 feet. The up-

right, spreading branches form a wineglass shape. Dark green foliage is held longer than other selections.

'Skyline' has fast growth to 40–45 feet and a pyramidal form. The leaves are dark green, compact, leathery, and larger than others.

'Sunburst' grows quickly to 30–35 feet with an upright, spreading habit. The new foliage is yellow, gradually turning green.

Grevillea robusta
Silk oak, silky oak

Evergreen
Zone 10
Native to Queensland and New South Wales, Australia.
Fast-growing to 50–60 feet, sometimes higher; and 20–35 feet wide; pyramidal in youth, eventually becoming round-topped.

Comblike, six- to ten-inch tresses of orange-yellow flowers, and coarsely fernlike leaves that are deep olive-green above and silver beneath, distinguish the silk oak, which is not a true oak at all. It is called silk oak because the wood, which has the grain and color of oak and was once used in cabinetmaking, has a definite sheen or silkiness when freshly cut.

Amazingly fast growth makes this an excellent temporary tree for use while permanent, stronger-wooded trees develop. This is a fine hedge, screen, or background plant that even grows well indoors. Silk oak likes well-drained soils, so it is a poor choice for a well-watered lawn. It can take drought and compacted soils. The bright golden orange flowers develop best in heat; it will flower poorly near the coast. Brittle wood makes it subject to wind damage, which is its main problem. Judicious pruning helps, but this also induces heavy suckering. The constantly dropping leaves can be a nuisance.

Hakea laurina
Sea urchin tree, pincushion tree

Evergreen
Zone 10
Native to Australia.
Moderate-growing to 25–30 feet; dense, round-headed.

This tree is valued for its ability to stand adversity, especially along the coast. The leaves are similar to some acacias—gray-green, long and narrow. The flowers, like crimson-gold pin cushions, appear in late fall and early winter. Widely adaptable to climate and soil, the sea urchin tree is also pest-free. It is useful as a small patio tree, hedge, or screen; it may need thinning in especially windy areas.

Halesia carolina
Snowdrop tree, wild olive

Deciduous
Zones 5–10
Native to the southeastern United States.
Slow- to moderate-growing to 25–30 feet; pyramidal in youth, round-headed with age.

This is one of the most attractive American natives. This pretty little tree is very popular in England and on the continent and is becoming more and more popular here in its country of origin; especially on the East coast. In mid-May, each twig bears a string of one-inch-long white flowers that resemble little wedding bells hanging down on slender stems. It's an open grower, usually in clump form with several stems; a fine shelter plant for combining with an underplanting of azaleas or rhododendrons.

Harpephyllum caffrum
Kaffir plum

Evergreen
Zone 10
Native to South Africa.
Fast-growing to about 30 feet tall and equally wide; round-headed; can be multi-trunked.

A well-behaved, fast-growing tree, useful for quick effects. The dark green, shiny leaves divided into 13 to 15 leaflets are its most attractive feature. It is tropical in appearance.

New growth is coppery-red. Insignificant white flowers are followed by dark-red, olive-like fruits that are edible but acidic. The growth habit becomes most picturesque with age.

Kaffir plum is easily pruned to any shape. It takes wind,

Grevillea robusta

Halesia carolina

Halesia carolina

Ilex aquifolium

Ilex cornuta

Ilex latifolia

Ilex opaca

Ilex vomitoria

coastal conditions, heat, and drought. A good choice for small garden, but fruit drop must be considered.

Ilex species
Holly

There are some 300 different species of hollies. They range from dwarf shrubs to 70-foot trees, and grow in the temperate and tropical regions of both hemispheres.

Some hollies have spiny leaves while other types have leaves with smooth margins. The fruit is black, red, yellow, or orange, depending upon the species or variety. Usually, both male and female plants are required to produce berries. One male will normally pollinate 16 to 19 females within 900 feet.

Most hollies thrive best on an acid soil. The trees will grow in full sunlight or partial shade but become leggy in dense shade.

English and American hollies are attacked by two kinds of leaf miners. The most common one makes blotches, the other a serpentine pattern. They are most active from April to mid-May. At that time, use Orthene®, dimethoate, diazinon, or a combination spray.

Scale and spider mites are sometimes a problem. Apply a dormant oil spray in winter to control overwintering mite eggs. Use Orthene® or a combination spray during the growing season.

Ilex aquifolium
English holly

Evergreen
Zones 7–10
Native to southern Europe and northern Africa.
Moderate-growing to 70 feet tall and 20 feet wide.

This is the holly used for Christmas decorations. Normally it has spiny, undulated, glossy, dark green leaves, but many silver and golden variegated forms have been named. Smooth-leafed forms and cultivars with spines on the leaf are available. Berry color varies from red to cream.

The following are some of the better cultivars.

'Angustifolia' has a narrow cone form with small narrow leaves. Usually the male form is available.

'Boulder Creek' is a California selection with very large, dark green, glossy leaves and heavy upright growth. The berries are a brilliant red.

'Little Bull,' a sport of 'Angustifolia,' has smaller leaves than the average *I. aquifolium*. It is a good pollenizer with a compact, upright habit that fits nicely into landscape plantings.

Ilex cornuta
Chinese holly

Evergreen
Zones 7–9
Native to China.
Grows to 15 feet tall as a shrub or small tree.

The large, spiny leaves are glossy and dark green. Large red berries develop on the female form.

Ilex latifolia
Luster-leaf holly

Evergreen
Zones 7–10
Native to eastern China and Japan.
Grows to 60 feet.

Luster-leaf holly has large, thick, leathery, glossy, sawtoothed leaves to 7 inches long and red berries. This holly should be planted on protected sites even in the South.

Ilex opaca
American holly

Evergreen
Zone 5–9
Native to the eastern United States.
Grows to 45–50 feet; pyramidal.

Through the use of hardy cultivars, this holly has been successfully grown north of its original home. Hardy cultivars have withstood temperatures of −24F° or even colder. The foliage is evergreen and the leaves are normally spiny. The color of the berries varies from red through orange to yellow, but the normal color is red.

When this tree is planted north of its original home it becomes more selective in the site requirements. In the southeast, American holly will grow on moist or wet sites. In the north, it requires good drainage and protection from severe winds.

Over a thousand selections of American holly have been named. Hardy red-berried forms include 'Angelica', 'Arlene Leach', 'Betty Pride', 'Carnival', 'Cumberland', 'Mary Holman', 'Red Flush', and 'Valentine'. 'Jersey Knight' and 'Santa Claus' are two hardy males. If you want yellow berries, plant 'Canary' or 'Morgan Gold'.

'Kentucky Smoothleaf' is a smooth-leafed variety that is somewhat tender, so plant in a protected location or in the southern states.

'East Palatka' is a southern smooth-leafed holly.

'Savannah' is another southern selection, prized for its heavy set of red berries.

Ilex vomitoria
Yaupon holly

Evergreen
Zones 7–10
Native to south Georgia.
Grows to 12–15 feet.

Yaupon holly can be used as a tall sheared hedge. It has small, shiny red berries and grows on wet sites.

Jacaranda acutifolia
Jacaranda

Deciduous
Zone 10
Native to Brazil.
Moderate- to fast-growing to 25–50 feet tall and two-thirds as wide; open, irregular head, often multitrunked.

One of the most beloved trees for warm climates, the Jacaranda tree flowers over a long period, usually from May to July. It is deciduous for only a short period. The interesting seed pods are attractive in dried displays.

This tree is tolerant of a variety of conditions, but becomes floppy with too much water; dwarfed with too little. It needs good drainage and is not advisable in high coastal winds. Extra training is necessary to develop its best form. A good choice for the garden or along the street.

Juglans species
Walnut

Almost 20 different species of these large, spreading trees are found in the temperate and tropical regions of the world. Many of these species provide lumber, shade, and edible nuts. In the United States two of the most common species are black walnut and Persian or English walnut.

Juglans nigra
Black walnut

Deciduous
Zones 4–8
Native to eastern United
  States and southeastern
  Canada.
Slow growing to 100–150 feet.

These large trees with their straight trunk and open, rounded crown are popular shade trees in large yards. The bark is thick and furrowed and becomes nearly black with age. The yellow-green leaves are 8 to 25 inches long and consist of 15 to 23 leaflets. The 1½ to 2½-inch long edible nuts are sweet and oily.

Juglans regia
Persian walnut, English walnut

Deciduous
Zones 6–10
Native from southeastern
  Europe to China.
Fast growing to 60–100 feet.

The Persian or English walnut tree is highly desirable for its edible nut crop. These are the walnuts most often found in mixed nuts or as packaged walnuts. This species is not desirable as a shade tree in spite of its large canopy. The fruit is messy and honeydew exudation from aphid infestations will stain patios, walkways, or cars beneath the tree.

Juniperus species
Juniper

This is a very large group of tough plants that range in size from low-spreading ground covers to tall columnar trees. Which juniper you choose depends on your climate. There is wide variety in the selections within the species. Here we look at two similar forms with different adaptations. Each is usually sold only by its various cultivars and is selected for blueness of foliage and a columnar growth habit.

Juniperus scopulorum
Rocky Mountain juniper

Needled evergreen
Zones 4–10
Native to the Rocky
  Mountains.
Slow-growing to 35–45 feet;
  broad pyramidal form
  becomes round-topped with
  age.

This is the best juniper for areas of heat and drought; a poor performer in areas of high summer rainfall or humidity. It has blue-gray foliage with brownish-red bark. An excellent choice as a tall hedge, screen, or windbreak.
  Many selections, varying in foliage color and form, are available.

Juniperus virginiana
Eastern red cedar

Needled evergreen
Zones 3–7
Native to eastern United
  States.
Slow-growing to 35–45 feet;
  pyramidal.

This eastern red cedar is adaptable to a remarkable range of soils and climates. Unlike *Juniperus scopulorum*, it will take summer rain, but not hot dry winds. Normally it has bright green foliage, but several selected varieties vary both in foliage color and form. It turns pinkish in cold winter weather and the attractive blue berries are a favorite winter bird food. Excellent as a long-lived tall hedge, screen, or windbreak.

Koelreuteria paniculata
Goldenrain tree, varnish tree

Deciduous
Zones 5–9
Native to China, Japan, and
  Korea.
Moderate-growing to 25–35
  feet; rounded outline, wide
  spreading open branches
  eventually developing to a flat
  top.

The goldenrain tree tolerates wind, alkaline soil, long periods without much water, and low temperatures in winter. It

Jacaranda acutifolia

Juglans regia

Koelreuteria paniculata

Laburnum watereri
'Vossii'

Lagerstroemia fauriei

Lagerstroemia indica

is a well-behaved tree although the branches tend to be brittle. The deep root system and the open branching habit permit grass to grow beneath the branches.

Starting in April, the new leaves develop quickly and cover the tree with soft, medium-green, divided leaves. By late spring or summer the flower spikes begin to open and the tree is completely covered with a mass of beautiful yellow flowers, enthusiastically visited by the honeybees. If the tree is kept watered, the flowers begin to set small fruits which develop an outer papery husk, very much like a husk tomato. Later in the summer, the fruits mature to a dark copper-tan and hang in clusters late into the fall.

Laburnum watereri
'Vossii'
Golden-chain tree

Deciduous
Zones 5–9
Hybrid of *Laburnum alpinum* and *Laburnum anagyroides*.
Moderate-growing to 20–30 feet; dense, upright, vase-shaped crown.

All observers agree that the only reason to choose this tree is for the flowers. In May it bears 18-inch, tapering clusters of rich yellow, pea-shaped flowers that look a good deal like wisteria blooms. It is not spectacular out of bloom. The leaves, fruits, and flowers are all very poisonous and it does not do well in very hot climates.

Lagerstroemia fauriei
Japanese crape myrtle

Deciduous
Zones 9–10
Native to Taiwan and China.
Slow-growing to 12–14 feet; vase-shaped.

This myrtle is very similar to *Lagerstroemia indica*, but with smaller white blossoms and no fall color. The bark is especially attractive, peeling brown and red.

The outstanding feature of this species is its resistance to powdery mildew, which makes it difficult to grow *Lagerstroemia indica* in cool, moist, coastal areas.

Lagerstroemia indica
Crape myrtle

Deciduous
Zones 8–10
Native to China.
Slow-growing to 10–30 feet.
Vase-shaped as a multi-trunked tree, round-headed when trained to a single stem.

Crape myrtle is best known for its late summer profusion of showy flowers in electric shades of pink, red, lavender, or white. The flowers are crinkled and ruffled like crepe-paper and held high above the foliage. The bark is attractive year-round, but especially in winter, when the peeling red and brown mottled trunk is quite striking. This is most dramatic on multitrunked trees. The fall color is good but inconsistent.

A hot dry climate is best because this myrtle will mildew in moist coastal locations.

The National Arboretum has introduced several cultivars of greater hardiness, mildew-resistance, and vigor, collectively called Indian Tribe Crape Myrtles. Notable selections include 'Catawba,' with good orange-red fall color and dark purple blossoms.

Lagunaria patersonii
Primrose tree, cow itch tree, sugarplum tree

Evergreen
Zones 9–10
Native to South Pacific, Australia.
Grows to 30–40 feet tall and 15 feet wide.

The so-called sugarplum tree is one of the few flowering trees that grows happily on the immediate coast. It develops into a fairly large, broad, pyramidal tree, producing many small pink blossoms, like hibiscus, to which it is related. Dense, gray-green foliage is salt- and wind-proof, which made it very popular for the beach a generation ago. Today it is almost forgotten. There is a potential hazard with this tree: Seed capsules are about 1 to 1½ inches long and (in addition to small black seeds) contain numerous fine bristles, like spun glass, which can cause unpleasant itching.

Larix leptolepis (L. kaempferi)
Japanese larch

Deciduous
Zones 5–8
Native to Japan.
Fast-growing to 50–60 feet tall and 25–40 feet wide; spreading pyramidal form.

This feathery conifer stands out from others by being deciduous and providing good fall color. It is broader and hardier than the European larch and has blue-green foliage, excellent yellow-orange fall color.

Laurus nobilis
Sweet bay, laurel bay, Grecian laurel

Evergreen
Zones 8–10
Slow-growing to 12–30 feet; compact conical form.

This is a well-behaved, indoor-outdoor tree. It has a very sophisticated look and takes well to shearing into hedges, screens, or formal shapes. The leaves are aromatic and dark green. The insignificant flowers are followed by small dark berries, which attract birds. Sweet bay stands city conditions; it requires well-drained soil, and works well as a wall tree.

Leptospermum laevigatum
Tea tree

Evergreen
Zones 9–10
Native to Australia.
Grows to 30 feet; artistically twisting, forms a beautiful canopy.

A rugged, sprawling tree with a trunk that takes on a sculptured form when mature. The leaves are stiff and grey. This tree does not need a lot of water. It makes a good specimen in the garden especially in the spring when tiny white, red, or pink flowers bloom.

Leucodendron argenteum
Silver tree

Evergreen
Zone 10
Native to South Africa.
Grows to 30–35 feet.

The silver tree is a genuine conversation piece. Lustrous, silky coated leaves are pure silver in appearance, about 3–4 inches long. They are sold as souvenir bookmarks in Capetown. This species is very particular about soil and exposure. It must have good drainage, hence open soil. A coastal influence is strongly recommended.

Ligustrum lucidum
Glossy privet

Evergreen
Zones 8–10
Native to China, Korea, and Japan.
Fast-growing to 35–40 feet tall and 15–20 feet wide, round-headed, often multitrunked.

The dense head, glossy, deep green foliage, and the ability to take shearing make this a very popular hedge or screen plant. Feathery clusters of milky white flowers in summer are followed by heavy clusters of small, berrylike, blue-black fruits. It tolerates salt winds and a wide variety of soils. A good tree for areas where root space is restricted. It makes a handsome container specimen. Glossy privet is useful as a small shade tree in a lawn or as a street tree, although the falling fruit may be messy.

Liquidambar styraciflua
American sweet gum

Deciduous
Zones 6–10
Native to the eastern and southern United States and Mexico.
Moderate- to slow-growing to 90 feet; a symmetrical pyramid when young, spreading to irregular with maturity.

The sweet gum is a reliable tree for autumn color. The star-shaped leaves, which resemble maple leaves, turn rich shades of crimson to purple in the fall. The color lasts as long as six weeks. The fruits, which mature in the fall, are the size of golf balls and are prickly like burrs. They may be a nuisance when they drop. The corky ridges on the branches give this tree winter interest. It is a good skyline tree.

This tree will grow on a wide variety of sites, but does best in rich clay or loam soils. It is

Larix leptolepis

Laurus nobilis

Ligustrum lucidum

Liquidambar styraciflua

Liquidambar styraciflua

Liriodendron tulipifera

Magnolia grandiflora

Magnolia acuminata

subject to chlorosis (yellowing of leaves) in heavy alkaline soils: addition of iron sulfate or chelates will help.

The symmetrical beauty of this genus is an asset to the home garden as well as being an excellent choice for a street tree.

The cultivars are selected for fall color.

'Burgundy' has purplish leaves that hold late into autumn.

'Festival' is a narrow upright tree with pink and orange fall color.

'Palo Alto' turns orange-red in fall.

Liriodendron tulipifera
Tulip tree, yellow poplar, tulip poplar

Deciduous
Zones 5–9
Native to the eastern United
    States.
Fast-growing, some have
    grown 60–70 feet in 70 years,
    tall pyramidal.

This is the tallest of the eastern hardwoods and needs plenty of room to develop properly. Its beauty lies in its uniquely shaped, bright green leaves that create a beautiful light canopy. It can look like a very clean sycamore from a distance. The fall color is yellow. Large, tulip-shaped, greenish-yellow flowers with an orange blotch at the base are borne in late spring. The flowers are best viewed up close, since they tend to blend into the foliage from a distance.

The wood has been found to be somewhat brittle and the roots can be invasive. The tulip tree does poorly in drought and alkaline soils.

This tree is best used in open areas, parks, and golf courses; it is a great skyline tree that can be grown in a large lawn.

Sooty mold and honeydew from aphids can become a problem on this tree. Do not use the tulip tree over a patio or parking area for this reason.

'Fastigiata' is a smaller cultivar that reaches only 35 feet with a narrow columnar form.

Magnolia species
Magnolia

Many gardeners have the idea that any tree that produces

such large exotic flowers on a bold-leafed plant must be difficult to grow. Not true. Even if you live in a climate one or two zones colder than the zone listed for the species, you might wish to try one of them if you have a suitably sheltered site. You may lose some flowers but the tree will be fine.

Magnolia species are frequently placed in one of three categories. One is the evergreen type, such as the southern magnolia. The second type is the deciduous magnolia that develops blooms after the leaves appear. The lily-flowered magnolia is one of these. The third group includes the type that flower before the leaves appear, such as the saucer magnolia. Some are variable, depending on where they are grown. The sweet bay magnolia is evergreen when it is grown in the South and deciduous when grown in the colder climates.

Magnolia acuminata
Cucumber tree

Deciduous
Zones 4–10
Native to the eastern United
    States.
Fast-growing to 50–80 feet
    tall and half as wide.

The most stately of the hardier magnolias, this is a vigorous tree that needs room to develop properly. The common name is derived from the shape and color of its fruit clusters.

Magnolia grandiflora
Southern magnolia

Evergreen
Zones 7–9
Native to the southern United
    States.
Moderate-growing to 60–75
    feet tall and 35–55 feet wide.

Magnolia grandiflora is a legend in the southern United States. To see the large (8 inches or more), fragrant, creamy white flowers and lustrous heavy-textured, 5–8 inch long leaves is to enjoy one of the world's finest flowering trees. The following are selected forms.

'St. Mary's' is a smaller tree (20 feet) known for its abundant bloom and predictable shape.

Magnolia soulangiana
Saucer magnolia

Deciduous
Zones 6–9
Native to the southeastern
  United States.
Moderate-growing to about
  20–30 feet tall and often
  equally wide.

Chances are that the saucer
magnolia is the most widely
planted and best known magnolia. It is a very popular
photographic subject. Colors
of the different varieties range
from white to dark reddish-
purple. Part of their popularity
is due to the fact that they
bloom well while still small.
They are sometimes planted
where a more erect-growing
tree should have been placed;
allow the space needed for
development of normal shape
or form.
  This is a hardy tree and
should not be planted in a
warm, sunny, protected spot.
This rushes the flowers'
development and they become
susceptible to late frost
damage. As for foliage, these
are not among the best-looking
magnolias after the flowers
have faded.

Magnolia stellata
Star magnolia

Deciduous
Zones 5–9
Native to Japan.
Moderate-growing to 25 feet
  with a rounded habit.

This tree is a beautiful sight,
when the fragrant white
flowers with strap-shaped
petals appear before the
leaves in late winter or early
spring. The flowers can be
damaged by frost, so avoid
southern exposures that
encourage buds to develop
early and flowers to open too
fast. This hardy, small tree
makes a good specimen plant.

Magnolia virginiana
Sweet bay magnolia

Deciduous or evergreen
Zones 5–9
Native to the southern and
  eastern United States.
In the North it grows to 10–20
  feet; in the South it can reach
  40–60 feet.

The sweet bay magnolia grows
as an evergreen in the south,
but is also one of the most popular magnolias in the colder
areas where it develops into a
tall deciduous shrub. It can
come close to suggesting a
miniature version of the southern magnolia with its smaller,
fragrant, creamy white, globu-
lar flowers and smaller (5-inch)
leaves, glossy above, blue-
white beneath. It blooms from
late spring to early fall on
favorable growing sites. Being
native to lowlands, it prefers
rich moist soil.

Malus species
Crabapple

More than 600 species and
varieties of flowering crabapples are being grown in the
United States and Canada. It is
the most widely adapted of the
flowering trees. Like all hardy
flowering fruits, it requires a
period of winter chilling and is
not adapted to the mild-winter
areas of the South and southern California.
  In some localities the tree's
resistance to apple scab is all-
important. In 1973 apple scab
was so serious in southeastern
Wisconsin that thousands of
trees were completely defoliated. In Massachusetts, New
Jersey, New York, Ohio,
Pennsylvania, Rhode Island,
and the District of Columbia,
annual surveys have been
made to determine which varieties are resistant to scab,
cedar apple rust, mildew, and
fireblight. Records of the surveys have been kept and constantly updated by Lester
Nichols of Pennsylvania State
University.
  Fireblight is a bacterial disease that survives in cankers,
leaves, and previously blight-
ed fruits. Usually it is spread
by insects during the bloom
period, gaining entry through
flowers and wounds. Symp-
toms are the sudden wilting of
leaves which then turn dark, as
if burned. Leaves hang on
rather than fall.
  A weak bordeaux, copper, or
streptomycin spray applied
during bloom will prevent the
disease. First spray when 10
percent of the flowers are
open, then continue repeating
every 5 to 7 days. Prune out
diseased wood, cutting several inches below the infected
parts into healthy wood. Ster-
ilizing pruning tools in a strong
solution of household bleach

Magnolia soulangiana

Magnolia virginiana

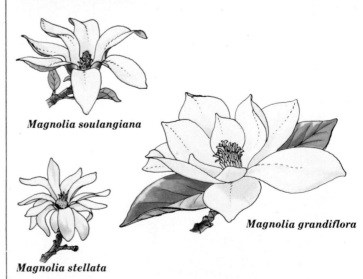

Magnolia soulangiana

Magnolia grandiflora

Magnolia stellata

Malus floribunda

Malus sargentii

Malus 'Van Eseltine'

Maytenus boaria

can prevent spreading the disease when pruning. Some of the most popular crabapples proved to be most susceptible and are not included. Noteworthy for their absence are 'Almey', 'Flame', 'Eleyi', and 'Hopa'.

In the following list we have noted those that have usable, good-sized fruit and are commonly used to make jams and jellies.

Malus baccata
Siberian crab

Deciduous
Zones 2–9
Native to Manchuria and
  China.
Grows to 15–30 feet;
  vase-shaped.

This tree is a heavy bearer and the fruit is usable. Fragrant, white flowers in early spring are followed by the 1–inch fruit. It is reasonably disease resistant.

Malus floribunda
*Japanese flowering
  crabapple*

Deciduous
Zones 7–9
Native to Japan.
Grows to 20 feet with a
  graceful arching spread.

Deep pink buds are pinkish-white in full flower, followed by small reddish-yellow fruit. Japanese flowering crabapple blooms profusely. It is resistant to scab but will get some fireblight.

Malus 'Red Jade'

Deciduous
Zones 4–8
Hybrid from undetermined
  crosses.
Slow-growing to 15–20 feet.

'Red Jade' gets its name from the color of its fruit. Small white flowers appear in great profusion on long, irregular, weeping branches in the spring. The heavy yield of usable fruit lasts late into the fall. It is reasonably disease-resistant, but will get some scab.

Malus sargentii
Sargent crabapple

Deciduous
Zones 4–8
Native to Japan.
Slow-growing to 8 feet.

Malus Sargentii has profuse clusters of small, white flowers that are fragrant. The flowers are followed by masses of small, dark-red fruit. This is a dwarf, spreading variety of crab apple with good disease resistance.

Malus 'Van Eseltine'

Deciduous
Zones 2–5
Cultivar of *Malus spectabilis*.
Grows to 18 feet;
  vase-shaped.

'Van Eseltine' flowers are borne in clusters. The buds are red, becoming pink as they open, and changing to white when fully open. The small, inedible fruits are golden yellow. This tree is resistant to scab, but susceptible to fireblight.

Malus zumi var. calocarpa

Deciduous
Zones 5–8
Cultivar from the cross of
  Malus baccata and *Malus
  seiboldii*.
Moderate-growing to 20 feet;
  pyramidal with weeping
  branchlets.

Malus zumi var. *calocarpa* has pink buds that open into fragrant, pure white flowers. Red fruit persists through the winter. This crabapple is resistant to scab, but will get some fireblight.

Maytenus boaria
Mayten tree

Evergreen
Zones 9–10
Native to Chile.
Slow-growing to 30–40 feet
  with a weeping habit.

Mayten tree takes heat and is tolerant of salinity in the soil. Useful in seaside plantings; it has interesting form and bark structure.

This is a great tree in mild climates. It is reminiscent of a willow without all the problems; has a cooling effect even in the hottest climates, and looks great off a patio or along a drive. Off the side of a sliding door or large window it will give a feeling of the outdoors becoming an extension of the indoors.

Malaleuca linariifolia
Snow-in-Summer, flaxleaf paperbark

Evergreen
Zones 9–10
Native to Australia.
Slow- to moderate-growing to 30 feet; narrow, upright, open when young; denser, round-headed with age.

Thin, pale-beige branchlets, with clusters of delicately pointed blue-green leaves, form an elegant contrast to the honey-brown papery bark peeling on the trunk and old limbs.
  In all seasons it is distinguished by its stylized texture and subtle coloring. *Malaleuca linariifolia* becomes truly spectacular in full bloom, during early summer, giving the effect of new-fallen snow (hence its common name).

Melia azedarach
Chinaberry

Deciduous
Zones 7–10
Native to Asia.
Fast-growing to 30–40 feet and equally wide; spreading umbrellalike crown.

A valuable tree for desert regions, this one has purple flowers followed by poisonous yellow berries. It sprouts suckers, drops berries, and has weak wood, but is useful where most trees won't grow.
  'Umbraculifera,' the Texas umbrella tree, is more common than the species. It has a tighter, more rounded umbrellalike form and is used in the desert.

Metasequoia glyptostroboides
Dawn redwood

Deciduous
Zones 5–8
Native to China.
Fast-growing to 80–100 feet.

The dawn redwood is a fossil age conifer that resembles the deciduous bald cypress in foliage character, although its flat needles are closer to the size of the hemlock, which is a northern tree. The trunk shape differs from bald cypress considerably. Dawn redwood has a buttress-shaped trunk; very wide at the base and deeply fluted bark that develops with age. Its

framework has a regular appearance with horizontal pendulous branches.
  The bark of the dawn redwood is reddish-brown with the twig bark somewhat orange-brown. The summer color is light green, turning yellow in the fall.

Metrosideros excelsus
New Zealand Christmas tree

Evergreen
Zone 10
Native to New Zealand.
Grows to 30 feet or more.

Metrosideros excelsus has a relatively short flowering period; red flowers appear in July, which coincides with Christmas in New Zealand. It is also called iron tree in New Zealand, where it develops a very thick trunk that cannot even be cut with an ax. The dark green leaves have fuzzy white undersides when mature. This tree needs to be pruned carefully or it will be more of a large shrub than a tree.

Nyssa sylvatica
Black tupelo, black gum, sour gum, pepperidge

Deciduous
Zones 5–9
Native to the eastern United States.
Moderate-growing rate to 30–50 feet tall and about half as wide.

In the wild, this tree, like the dogwood, grows along river banks and on floodplains. Its lovely scarlet, glossy, autumn leaves look marvelous against the foliage of evergreens.
  Black tupelo develops a dense canopy of beautiful, deep glossy green foliage.
  The mountain people in the Alleghenies use a twig as a toothbrush—when chewed, the twig frays into a nice little brush. The spring buds make a red patch in the woods and the naked winter branches make a lovely silhouette against the sky.

Olea europaea
Olive

Evergreen
Zones 9–10
Native to the Mediterranean countries and western Asia.

Melia azedarach

Melia azedarach

Metasequoia glyptostroboides

Nyssa sylvatica

Olea europaea

Ostrya virginiana

Oxydendrum aboreum

Paulownia tomentosa

Fairly fast-growing in youth, slowing down with age, to 20–30 feet; rounded head.

The olive's gray-green leaves with silvery undersides and attractive gnarled gray trunk are seen throughout California. This is one of the easiest trees to transplant when old and mature.

If the fruits are not to be consumed, they are a nuisance when they drop on paving or any area with heavy traffic. The fallen fruits will harm a lawn, and must be raked up. Scale is sometimes a problem on olives.

Several cultivars are available.

'Swan Hill' is fruitless, so it makes a desirable and good-looking street tree on wide avenues.

'Ascolano' is the most attractive fruiting variety and is grown commercially. The large fruits are tender, and should be handled with care if you intend to preserve them.

'Manzanillo' has a stiffer branching habit than 'Ascolano,' and is less desirable for home planting. Its large fruits are also good for oil and for preserving, and are not as tender as those of 'Ascolano.'

Ostrya virginiana
American hop hornbeam

Deciduous
Zones 4–9
Slow-growing to 30–35 feet, round-headed tree.

This small, graceful tree has little problem with pests or diseases. The attractive bark of the trunk and larger branches has long frayed, platelike strips. The foliage is medium green, developing a fair reddish autumn color. American hop hornbeam is somewhat difficult to transplant, but is tolerant of a wide range of soils. It has done quite well under adverse inner-city conditions.

Oxydendrum arboreum
Sourwood

Deciduous
Zones 5–9
Native to the eastern United States.
Slow-growing to 30–40 feet; pyramidal.

The common name, sourwood, comes from the very sour-tasting foliage. This tree requires acid soil and no competition from lawn or other plants.

There have been many arguments as to which is our most beautiful native American small flowering tree. Many insist it is the white dogwood, but others hold out for the sourwood. It is constantly a beauty, starting with the translucent amber red of the young leaves as they unfold in the spring, continuing with the big, pendulous sprays of white flowers borne for a long period in July, and finishing with the brilliant scarlet color of the foliage in autumn. The sourwood is light and feathery, looking more like an oriental tree than a shade tree. Its delicate and enduring beauty is best enjoyed at close hand near a terrace or patio.

Parrotia persica
Persian parrotia

Deciduous
Zones 6–9
Native to Iran.
Slow-growing to 30–40 feet tall and 15–30 feet wide; oval habit with upsweeping branches.

Persian parrotia is an excellent, pest-free, small specimen tree. It is colorful in all seasons but most spectacular in the fall when the dark green leaves turn from bright yellow to orange and finally to scarlet. In the winter the attractive bark is flakey with white patches beneath. The new spring leaves are reddish purple as they unfold.

Paulownia tomentosa
Empress tree

Deciduous
Zones 7–10
Native to China.
Fast-growing to 40–60 feet tall and equally wide, with a rounded head.

The spectacular empress tree thrives in full sun and rich, well-drained soil. It tolerates city pollution but does not do well in hot, dry conditions.

Vanilla scented, pale violet flowers appear before the leaves, sometime in April. They are 2 inches long, trumpet shaped and held in 1 foot clusters. If temperatures are very warm or very cold the tree does not flower well. This is a good tree where there is plenty of space, as in a park. The dense shade makes it almost impossible to grow grass or other plants underneath.

Phellodendron amurense
Amur corktree

Deciduous
Zones 4–9
Native to China and Japan.
Moderate-growing to 30–50 feet tall and even wider spread.

The amur corktree has glossy foot-long, dark green, compound leaves. The bark develops an attractive and unusual corky texture that is gray-black in color.

This tree is pest-free and tolerant of both pollution and drought. The shallow root system prohibits its use along streets or in lawns but it makes a good light shade tree, especially suited to parks or other large areas.

Picea species
Spruce

Most of the spruce of North America are native to the northern areas of the continent: Canada, Alaska, and the northern parts of the United States from Minnesota and Wisconsin to New England. In fact, you could name the colors of the American flag with spruce trees: Some of the species have the common names red spruce, white spruce, and blue spruce.

Spruce and red spider mites and the Cooley spruce gall aphid are common spruce pests. The mites are colored dark green to black or red, produce copious amounts of webbing, and turn the tree grayish. Control them with Orthene®.

Cooley spruce gall aphids cause conelike galls to form at ends of twigs. Galls are green to reddish-purple in spring, then turn brown, dry and hard in summer. Spray dimethoate, diazinon, or other insecticides labeled for this pest.

There is a simple trick to identifying spruce trees. The

needles (leaves) of nearly all spruce are squarish in cross-section and can be rolled between the thumb and index finger. Fir and hemlock needles are flattish and do not roll easily like those of spruce. Spruce also differ from fir by having cones that hang downward rather than standing straight up, and the cones remain intact when they fall rather than shattering.

Picea abies
Norway spruce

Evergreen
Zones 3–8
Native to Europe.
Fast-growing and columnar to 100–150 feet.

The most widely adapted spruce, the Norway spruce is not a United States native. It was brought from Europe early in this country's history.

These beautiful pyramidal evergreens are more attractive as they age, because the branchlets gradually become more pendulous. Norway spruce makes an excellent windbreak and tall screen. One characteristic that has made them so popular is their natural ability to retain their lower branches and needles.

Where space permits, Norway spruce is a good landscape specimen. Do not plant on poor sites; avoid dry ridges and slopes where soils are likely to be low in fertility. Preferred sites are cool and moist. Hot weather weakens this tree. Besides all its other fine features, there are the very large (for a spruce) and attractive seed-bearing cones, 4–7 inches long.

Norway spruce has produced many unusual forms that range from dwarf to weeping, and from compact to spreading. Many, especially the weeping forms, will require staking to bring them up to the desired height.

Picea glauca
White spruce

Deciduous
Zones 3–4
Native to Alaska, Canada, and the northern United States.
Moderate-growing to 50–80 feet; conical with drooping branchlets.

The white spruce is extremely hardy, withstanding both very cold and very hot, dry conditions. Although it is a large tree, there are two popular compact forms.

Picea glauca 'Densata', Black Hills spruce, is a slow grower.

Picea glauca 'Conica' also grows slowly and has a formal character.

Picea omorika
Serbian spruce

Evergreen
Zones 4–8
Native to southern Europe.
Moderate growth to 60–100 feet with a columnar, slender habit and upturned branch tips.

This spirelike spruce deserves much wider use than its availability would indicate. The glossy, dark green needles are borne on a slender-trunked tree with short ascending branches, and a very narrow pyramidal head like that of the Norway spruce. The tree usually retains its lower branches, a most valuable trait in a specimen tree that is expected to retain its beauty throughout its lifetime. For its height, no spruce is likely to use less ground area. This fact permits it to be used on small landscapes where other *Piceas* would not be suitable.

Picea pungens
Colorado spruce

Evergreen
Zones 3–8
Native to Wyoming, Utah, Colorado, and New Mexico.
Will grow 80–100 feet with time; stiff pyramidal form with dense, horizontal branches.

As a young tree, the Colorado spruce is beautiful, vigorous, and fast-growing, but its growth slows with age. Its major fault is its tendency to lose its lower branches, detracting from its beauty as a mature tree. Nurseries propagate several forms with pronounced whitish-blue needles. Most likely to be available are the varieties 'Koster,' 'Moerheimii,' and 'Hoopsii.' Some horticulturalists feel these bluish types are so different that they require careful placement in a landscape; otherwise their colors will dominate, even to their own disadvantage.

Phellodendron amurense

Picea abies

Picea abies

Picea pungens 'Koster'

Picea omorika

Pinus bungeana

Pinus canariensis

Pinus coulteri

Pinus densiflora

Picea sitchensis
Sitka spruce

Evergreen
Zones 6–9
Native to Alaska through
  California.
Fast-growing to 100–150 feet;
  develops from a conical shape
  into the mature form, which
  is a broad pyramid.

Sitka spruce is the tallest
known spruce and an extremely rapid grower. It grows best
along the coast where the
climate stays cool and humid.

Pinus species
Pine

Of the more than one hundred
species of pines in the world,
over 40 are native to North
America. These evergreens
vary widely, from slow-
growing trees suitable for container planting to picturesque,
wind-shaped pines of the
Pacific Coast, to the majestic
hardy pines of the lumber
forests. They are used in patio
containers and shaped into
bonsai trees. In the garden
they are used for shade, as
specimen trees, for wind-
breaks, and as tall hedges.
Pines fill a variety of needs.
  The individual species of pine
are identified by the size and
number of needles that are
held in each bundle and by the
appearance of the cones.

Pinus aristata
Bristlecone pine

Evergreen
Zones 5–7
Native to the mountains of
  Colorado through California.
Slow-growing to 45 feet.

Needles are 5 in a bundle,
1–1½ inches long, usually
flecked with white dots of
resin. They will remain on
twigs 20 to 30 years, giving the
ends of the branches a bushy
or brushlike appearance. The
cones are 3½ inches long. A
bristlecone pine may only
average 3 inches increase in
height a year. Some specimens
in the mountains of the southwestern United States are
approaching 5000 years old—
the oldest living trees in the
world. They will grow on very
dry and exposed sites. Use
this dwarf and picturesque
pine as a specimen or in a rock
garden where years will pass
before it outgrows its space.

Pinus bungeana
Lacebark pine

Evergreen
Zones 5–9
Native to northwest China.
Slow-growing to 75 feet.

The needles are 3 in a bundle,
3 inches long, and usually
dense. The cones are 2 to 3
inches long. The bark is most
interesting when it is scaling
off, leaving chalky, white
patches. Lacebark pine holds
its needles 5 years or longer.
Often it is spreading and picturesque, with several trunks.
This is an overlooked but very
desirable pine that works well
as a specimen plant.

Pinus canariensis
Canary Island pine

Evergreen
Zones 8–10
Native to the Canary Islands.
Fast-growing to 60–80 feet,
  pyramidal and upright.

The blue-green foliage of a
young tree turns darker green
with age. It naturally clears
itself of lower branches,
making it a good shade tree.
This beautiful tree is also
drought tolerant.

Pinus coulteri
Coulter pine

Evergreen
Zones 7–9
Native to California.
Moderate- to fast-growing to
  30–80 feet.

The lower branches of the
coulter pine spread wide to the
ground and persist, which
makes it useful as a screen or
for erosion control. It does
well on dry, hot rocky mountain slopes and tolerates wind.
Coulter pine becomes more
symmetrical with age, but it is
too large for the small garden.

Pinus densiflora
Japanese red pine

Evergreen
Zones 5–9
Native to Japan.
Fast-growing to 50–60 feet
  and equally wide.

The Japanese red pine usually
forms two or more trunks at
ground level and has attractive
reddish bark. The branches
spread horizontally and the
tree has an open, loose habit.
It can be dwarfed.

Pinus echinata
Shortleaf pine

Evergreen
Zones 6–9
Native to New York through
 Florida and to Texas.
Grows to 100 feet.

The needles of the shortleaf
pine are held 2 in a bundle,
sometimes 3 on young trees,
and 3 to 5 inches long. The
cones are 1½–2 inches long.
This is the most widespread
of the southern yellow pines.
It grows in coastal plains,
Piedmont areas, and in the
mountains up to 2000 feet in
elevation; growth is poor
above 2000 feet. The shortleaf
pine grows naturally in dense
stands and will grow on a great
variety of soils. It has been
extensively planted in reforestation projects. Generally
available as a container plant
for landscaping, it makes a
handsome lawn tree.

Pinus elliottii
Slash pine

Evergreen
Zones 8–9
Native to the southeastern
 United States.
Fast-growing to 100 feet.

The needles of slash pine are
held 2 or 3 in a bundle, 5–10
inches long. Cones are 4–6
inches long. The fastest growing of the southern yellow
pines, it may grow to be 20
feet tall in 5 years. Its growth
is confined to the coastal plain.
Planting has extended its original range to eastern Texas
and north into Virginia. It
grows on sandy sites and will
grow on wetter, poorer-
drained sites than most pines.
The rich green color and
branching habit make this tree
a desirable landscape
ornament.

Pinus glabra
Spruce pine

Evergreen
Zones 8–9
Native to the southeastern
 United States.
Grows to 100 feet.

Cones 1½–2½ inches long.
Spruce pine grows naturally in
damp coastal woods such as
swamps and river bottoms.
This is a low-branching tree
when young. The branches
droop, making it an attractive

specimen tree. When young,
use the spruce pine as a screen
planting.

Pinus lambertiana
Sugar pine

Evergreen
Zones 6–7
Native to Oregon through Baja
 California.
Slow-growing for the first
 5 years; eventually grows to
 200 feet or more.

This is the world's tallest pine.
Old trees are usually flat-
topped with an open, spreading head. The blue-green
needles are 3–4 inches long
and held in bundles of 5. The
cones are 12–20 inches long.
Sugar pine becomes more
beautiful with age, and it is a
good specimen tree.

Pinus monophylla
Single-leaf pinyon pine

Evergreen
Zones 6–7
Native to Idaho through to
 California and down to
 Mexico.
Very slow-growing to
 10–25 feet, with a small
 round head.

The gray-green needles are
carried singly and are about 1
inch long. The round cones are
2 inches long. Single-leaf
pinyon pine is symmetrical and
narrow-crowned as a young
tree, but as a mature tree it
has a short, crooked trunk that
is often divided. This pine
provides delicious pine nuts.
The nut pine (*Pinus edulis*) is
similar but more irregular in
growth habit, and should be
grown in containers.

Pinus nigra
Austrian pine

Evergreen
Zones 4–8
Native to central and southern
 Europe and Asia Minor.
Moderate-growing to 60–80
 feet in height, but can grow to
 100 feet; at maturity it
 becomes flat topped, but is
 densely pryamidal and wide-
 spreading in youth.

The sharp, stiff needles of
Austrian pine are held 2 in
a bundle, 4–8 inches long.
The oval cones grow to about
3 inches long.
An important pine in the
East, this pine is tolerant of

moist, but not wet, soils and
city conditions. It can be used
as a specimen tree or a screen
and will withstand winter cold
and wind.

Pinus palustris
Longleaf pine

Evergreen
Zones 7–9
Native to Virginia through
 Florida and to Mississippi.
Grows to 125 feet.

Needles held 3 in a bundle,
8–15 inches long. The cones
are 6–12 inches long. The
longleaf pine is mostly confined
to deep sandy soils with good
drainage. It grows poorly on
heavy soils. The seedlings
remain with their terminal bud
at ground level for 5–7 years in
the so-called "grass stage"
while developing a tap root.
This is one of the four southern
yellow pines producing high-
grade lumber. Longer-lived
than most southern pines, it is
an interesting tree with a trunk
that eventually becomes free
of branches. The extensive
taproot makes transplanting
somewhat difficult.

Pinus parviflora
Japanese white pine

Evergreen
Zones 6–7
Native to Japan.
Slow-growing to 90 feet.

The needles of the Japanese
white pine are 5 in a bundle,
1½–2½ inches long. The
cones are 2–3 inches long and
can remain on the tree for 6–7
years. Japanese white pine will
grow in zone 5 on protected
sites. The crown can spread
almost as wide as the tree
is tall, so give it ample room
to develop. This excellent
specimen tree should be more
widely used. It grows on sandy
loam to silty clay.
 'Glauca,' silver Japanese
white pine, has needles that
are silver-blue. This is a more
striking tree than the species.

Pinus pungens
Table Mountain pine

Evergreen
Zones 5–8
Native to New Jersey
 through Georgia.
Slow-growing to 20–50 feet.

The stiff, dark green needles
of the Table Mountain pine are

Pinus elliottii

Pinus monophylla

Pinus palustris

Pinus parviflora

Pinus pungens

Pinus radiata

Pinus sabiniana

Pinus strobus

held on spreading branches that often form an irregular or flat-topped crown. They are 2–3 inches long and hold 2–3 needles to a bundle. The 3–4 inch cones stay on the tree for several years. This scrub pine is good in a large container.

Pinus radiata
Monterey pine

Evergreen
Zones 8–10
Native to California through Baja California.
Fast-growing to 60–100 feet.

The 3–7 inch needles are held 2–3 in a bundle and clusters of 3–5 inch cones stay on the tree for many years. The Monterey pine is normally pyramidal but develops a rounded, flattish crown with age and is often contorted by the wind. Use it for windbreaks, screens, and large hedges.

Pinus sabiniana
Digger pine

Evergreen
Zones 8–10
Native to California.
Fast-growing to 40–50 feet.

The main trunk of the digger pine divides into secondary trunks. The mature tree has an open crown and lacy gray-green foliage. The needles are 8–12 inches long with 3 to a bundle. The oval cones grow up to 10 inches long. The edible nuts of this tree once provided food for the Digger Indians.

Pinus strobus
White pine

Evergreen
Zones 2–8
Native to eastern North America.
Grows to 150 feet.

The needles of the white pine are 5 in a bundle, 3–5 inches long. The cones are 4–5 inches long. In the forest, this pine has been known to grow 200 feet tall. White pine grows best on well-drained sandy loams or silty soils but it will grow on most soils. This long-lived tree can survive to 450 years or more. In southern mountains it grows to elevations of 4000 feet or higher. This tree has been widely planted in reforestation projects and as an ornamental; it is often used as a screen. A number of horticultural cultivars have been developed for special planting situations. The following are two of the most common.

'Nana,' dwarf white pine, is very compact and grows 6–10 feet tall with a spread of 10 feet or more.

'Pendula,' weeping white pine, has branches that droop and touch the ground.

Pinus sylvestris
Scotch pine, Scots pine

Evergreen
Zones 3–8
Native to Eurasia.
Grows to 75 feet.

Twisted, green needles of the Scotch pine are borne 2 in a bundle, 1½–3 inches long. The cones are 2 inches long. The bark is reddish-orange in color at first, maturing to a grayish red-brown. Scotch pines are planted as Christmas trees and specimen trees. This is quite a variable species and many strains and cultivars have been developed.

Pinus taeda
Loblolly pine

Evergreen
Zones 7–9
Native to New Jersey through Texas.
Grows to 100 feet.

The needles of this tree are 3 in a bundle and 6–8 inches long. Although loblolly pine grows on poorly drained sites, it does poorly on excessively drained sandy sites. It has been widely planted as a source of timber and pulpwood. When grown in the open, this tree develops a good crown and makes an excellent shade tree.

Pinus thunbergiana
Japanese black pine

Evergreen
Zones 5–8
Native to Japan.
Fast-growing to 90 feet.

The needles of Japanese black pine are borne 2 in a cluster, 3–4 inches long. The cones are 2–3 inches long. Large, white terminal buds help to identify this tree. It is one of the best evergreens for seashore planting. Japanese black

pine is planted as a specimen tree in the mountains. The crown becomes irregular and spreading as it approaches maturity.

Pinus virginiana
Virginia pine

Evergreen
Zones 5–8
Native to New York through Georgia and Alabama.
Grows to 50 feet, occasionally to 90.

The needles are 2 in a bundle, twisted and 1–3 inches long. The cones are 1–2 inches long. Virginia pine is usually a short-lived, shallow-rooted, scrubby tree that retains its old cones for years until the crown is full of them. It is an old field pine that often seeds in almost pure stands on abandoned bare land.

Pinus wallichiana (P. griffithii)
Himalayan pine

Evergreen
Zones 6–7
Native to the Himalayas.
Grows to 50–80 feet, can reach 150 feet in some cases; broad, conical form.

The needles of this tree are held 5 in a bundle, 6–8 inches long. The cones are 6–10 inches long. Long, drooping, blue-green needles are most attractive. Himalayan pine grows best on sandy loam. It resembles native white pine but the needles and cones are usually longer. Grow this tree as a specimin but give it room to develop a spread of 40 feet or more.

Pistacia chinensis
Chinese pistachio

Deciduous
Zones 6–10
Native to China.
Moderate-growing to 50–60 feet tall and equally wide; spreading umbrellalike crown.

This is one of the best trees for filtered shade. The bright green leaves grow up to 12 inches long and are divided into graceful leaflets. The new leaves have a pink tinge, turning brilliant shades of yellow to orange and red in fall. The zigzag branching pattern is quite attractive.

Pinus sylvestris

Pinus thunbergiana

Pinus wallichiana

Pistacia chinensis

Pittosporum tobira

Pittosporum undulatum

Platanus acerifolia

Widely adapted, Chinese pistachio grows best with summer heat. An excellent lawn or street tree, although the female tree will produce berries when a male tree is nearby. There are no disease problems. Because of its uneven growth habit, a little extra pruning may be needed when the tree is young to develop good form.

Pittosporum species
Pittosporum

Pittosporum are mild climate plants that break down into two groups: the hedge-forming plants and those species that are best left standing alone as small garden or patio trees. Differences between species lie in the size, shape, and color of the leaf and the resulting texture of the canopy. Only the tree types are discussed here.

Pittosporum phillyraeoides
Willow pittosporum

Evergreen
Zones 9–10
Native to Australia.
Grows to 15–20.

The trailing branches of willow pittosporum have narrow, 3-inch-long, dusty green leaves. This is a unique weeping form.

Pittosporum rhombifolium
Queensland pittosporum

Evergreen
Zones 9–10
Native to eastern Australia.
Grows to 20–35 feet.

Diamond-shaped, 4-inch-long, glossy green leaves and showy fruits characterize this willow pittosporum. It is often used as a screen.

Pittosporum tobira
Japanese pittosporum, mock orange

Evergreen
Zones 8–10
Native to China and Japan.
Slow-growing to 18 feet.

This durable plant is much better known as a foundation shrub, but it can be coaxed upward on one or several trunks to a patio-size tree. Its slow growth rate means that it will never outgrow patio proportions. Small, sweetly fragrant off-white flowers are produced in profusion in spring.

Pittosporum undulatum
Victorian box

Evergreen
Zones 9–10
Native to Australia.
Grows up to 40 feet high.

The glossy 5-inch green leaves have wavy edges; the fruit is sticky. It is a useful tree for a tall screen.

Platanus acerifolia
London plane tree

Deciduous
Zones 5–9
Hybid of *Platanus occidentalis* and *Platanus orientalis*.
Fast-growing to 40–60 feet; open spreading crown.

This versatile and widely adapted tree can take harsh city conditions, drought, and tough soils. A London plane tree is often pollarded—a technique of severe pruning. It is widely used as a street tree and in malls. The large-lobed leaves are bright green; the brown, ball-shaped fruits are borne 2 to a cluster. The most attractive feature is the striking green and white flaking bark; there is no fall color. To some observers, the bark gives the impression of dappled sunlight. Of all the sycamores, it is the most resistant to anthracnose.

Podocarpus macrophyllus
Yew pine

Evergreen
Zones 8–10
Native to Japan.
Slow-growing to 50–60 feet; erect, columnar form.

A valuable indoor-outdoor plant with a graceful oriental character. Long, narrow, rather stiff bright green leaves grow on slightly drooping branches. Yew pine is pest-free and widely adapted, but it may show chlorosis in alkaline or heavy soils. Protected locations will extend its hardiness. It is a great tree to plant along entryways or to use in containers; it also makes a fine hedge or espalier.

Populus species
Poplar

Few trees hardy in temperate zones grow as rapidly as poplars. An unrooted cutting, spring-planted in an area of rich soil and abundant moisture, can reach 12 or more feet in height by the following autumn. Although such fantastic growth slows down as the tree grows older, it is still unique among hardy trees. This rapid growth rate, coupled with tolerance of a wide variety of soil types and the production of wood with definite industrial value, has led to considerable interest in poplars for reforestation.

In some very arid areas of the West, locally native poplars are among the few trees that will survive and grow large enough to provide shade. Of these adapted species, male trees that do not produce clouds of cottonlike seed, such as 'Siouxland,' the cottonless cottonwood, are much to be preferred over ordinary seedlings. Another important use for poplars, particularly the narrow-growing varieties, is for quick-growing screening to hide unsightly areas and buildings or to make windbreaks. When there is enough room, the ideal solution to a screening problem is to plant a row of the very rapid-growing but short-lived Lombardy poplars adjacent to a row of arbovitae, spruce, or narrow junipers. By the time the poplars begin to decline, the evergreens are tall enough to do the screening job.

Populus alba
White poplar

Deciduous
Zones 4–10
Native to Europe and Asia.
Rapid-growing to
    50–90 feet.

This tall and wide-spreading species is very hardy and its foliage is among the prettiest of all poplars. The leaves resemble small maple leaves, dark green above and silvery white underneath; they are especially attractive on a breezy day. White poplar grows exceptionally well at the seashore, being highly resistant to salt spray and even

temporary immersion of the root area. Its great fault is the persistent sprouting of shoots from the wide-spreading root system. But it is quite useful by the seashore in poor, sandy soils where few trees will grow at all.

'Pyramidalis,' the Bollcana poplar, has the fine foliage of the white poplar but is well suited for screening purposes. Fortunately, it does not sprout from the roots like the wild type.

Populus nigra 'Italica'
Lombardy poplar

Deciduous
Zones 2–6
Fast-growing to 90 feet;
    columnar.

The handsome Lombardy poplar is one of the oldest known varieties of ornamental trees. It is unbeatable as a tall screen or accent tree in every respect but one—it is very susceptible to stem canker disease as it reaches maturity. There is great variation in disease incidence, the general rule being that Lombardy poplars grow better and healthier the farther north they are planted. There are some places (such as around Seattle, Washington) where they do exceptionally well. Elsewhere, the tree is still useful for "instant screening," with the knowledge that there may be disease losses after 15 to 20 years of vigorous growth.

Populus nigra thevestina, Theves poplar or Algerian poplar, is a similar variety that is said to be much more canker resistant. It has white bark and grows broader than the Lombardy poplar.

Populus simonii
'Fastigiata'

Deciduous
Zones 2–6
Native to China.
Fast-growing to 35 feet;
    narrow pyramidal.

This beautiful, narrow tree is a variety of one of the most hardy of all poplars, from the harsh climate of northern China. It has pretty, reddish branchlets bearing shiny, bright green leaves. It reaches approximately 45 feet in height at maturity and, while not as

narrow as a Lombardy poplar, it is still much taller than it is broad and makes a fine, quick-growing screening plant. In addition to its other good qualities, it is very resistant to canker disease, which guarantees a long life. It does not sucker from the roots.

Prosopis glandulosa torreyana
Mesquite

Deciduous
Zones 7–9
Native to the southwestern
    United States.
Grows to 30 feet with loose-
    spreading crown; usually
    multitrunked.

This is a tree for hot, dry regions. The gray-green foliage casts filtered shade. Greenish-yellow flowers in spring and summer attract bees. Mesquite is drought-tolerant and takes alkaline soils. It can be used as a screen or windbreak.

Prunus species

This genus comprises over 400 species and numerous cultivars of trees and shrubs growing in temperate climates —mostly in the Northern Hemisphere.

This group includes all the stone fruits: almonds, apricots, cherries, nectarines, peaches, and plums. These fruit trees are grown for their edible fruits and, in many cases, are also highly ornamental. The following entries are divided into three groups: the cherries, the plums, and the evergreen laurels. The cherries and plums are discussed in detail in the Ortho book *All About Fruits & Berries.*

Cherries

The cherries can be divided into three groups: the European, the American, and the Oriental. In general, the Oriental types are less hardy than the others.

Prunus avium
Sweet cherry

Deciduous
Zones 4–8
Native to Europe and Asia.
Fast-growing to 50 feet.

The attractive bark of the

Populus alba

Populus nigra 'Italica'

Prunus avium

Prunus sargentii

Prunus serrulata

Prunus virginiana 'Shubert'

sweet cherry matures to a mahogany red and the flowers are white. This is the ancestor of most sweet cherries. It can be planted where oriental cherries are not hardy. 'Plena,' Mazzard cherry, is a white cultivar. The double flowers have up to 30 petals and they bloom a week before the double-flowered orientals. Sweet cherries have been cultivated for two and a half centuries.

Prunus ilicifolia
Hollyleaf cherry

Evergreen
Zones 9–10
Native to the California coast and Baja California.
Moderate-growing to 12–35 feet.

Hollyleaf cherry has dark green hollylike leaves. The new growth is lighter green and adds a soft look to the tree. The small clusters of attractive white flowers are followed by edible red cherries that gradually turn to a deep reddish-purple.

Prunus sargentii
Sargent cherry

Deciduous
Zones 5–9
Native to northern Japan, Korea, and the Sakhalin peninsula.
Moderate-growing to 50 feet.

This is the hardiest of oriental cherries. The deep pink flowers bloom before the double Japanese cherries. This beautiful tree has a long list of assets: It is hardy, has good fall color, attractive bark, and matures into one of the largest oriental cherries.

Prunus serotina
Black cherry

Deciduous
Zones 4–9
Native to Nova Scotia through North Dakota and south to Florida and Texas.
Moderate-growing to 90 feet.

This native species has fragrant white flowers in clusters 2–6 inches long. The fruit is black and especially relished by birds, although it is not a favorite with people. When grown in the open as a specimen, it develops a huge, rounded crown. The branches are partially drooping.

Prunus serrulata
Japanese flowering cherry

Deciduous
Zones 6–9
Native to eastern Asia.
Grows to 20–25 feet.

The attractive habit of this cherry is further enhanced when the fragrant, white double flowers bloom in the spring. Over 120 cultivars have been developed. *Prunus serrulata* is one of the two types of cherries in the famous Washington, D.C. plantings.

'Amanogawa' cherry grows to 20 feet and is the most narrow and upright of the Japanese cherries. The flowers are pale pink.

'Kwanzan,' the most popular and hardy of the double-flowered oriental cherries, grows to 12–18 feet and has deep-pink flowers.

Prunus subhirtella
Higan cherry

Deciduous
Zones 6–8
Native to Japan.
Grows to 25 feet tall and equally wide.

Higan cherry blooms early in the spring with a large, showy display of pink flowers. This tree is intolerant of city conditions and smog.

Prunus virginiana
Chokecherry

Deciduous
Zones 2–9
Native to North America.
Grows 20–30 feet tall and 15–25 feet wide.

Variety 'Shubert' has red leaves that last all summer. The black fruits against the red foliage are quite striking.

Prunus yedoensis
Yoshino cherry

Deciduous
Zones 6–8
Native to Japan.
Fast-growing to 40 feet; flat-topped, wide spreading.

Yoshino cherry is one of the most rapid-growing cherries. Single white flowers are borne in abundance early in the season. This cherry comprises the main part of the cherry display in the Washington, D.C. tidal basin.

Plums

The plums, like cherries, include three varieties: American, Euroasiatic, and Sino Japanese. Most plums have heavy spring blooms and furnish edible fruit as well. Plum trees can be mere shrubs or small trees that seldom exceed 30 feet in height. Some plums also form thickets.

The flowering plums can be divided into two groups. Some bear edible fruit annually, others bear fruit seldom or not at all and are selected for their foliage and flowers. Your choice between the two groups depends upon where you plant and your point of view. Near sidewalks, fruit drop can be annoying. Planted where the fruits can be picked, the trees are appreciated. A number of plums require two seedling trees or two different varieties for cross pollination to obtain a good set of fruit.

Prunus cerasifera
Cherry plum

Deciduous
Zones 4–8
Native to central Asia through the Balkans.
Grows to 25 feet tall and equally wide.

Cherry plum flowers are white, and the yellow or reddish fruit is quite sweet.

Evergreen Laurels

The cherry laurels, or laurel cherries, are grown for their attractive evergreen foliage. The fruit is small and is eaten by birds. These plants are used as hedges, screens, backgrounds, and as specimens.

Prunus caroliniana
Cherry laurel

Evergreen
Zones 7–10
Native to North Carolina through Texas.
Grows 18–40 feet.

Cherry laurel is a large shrub or a small tree that often forms a dense thicket. The trunk diameter can reach 1 foot. The plant has been widely spread by birds who favor the ½-inch black fruit. The flowers are white, relatively free from insects and disease, and can stand heavy shearing.

Prunus lusitanica
Portugal laurel

Evergreen
Zones 7–10
Native to Spain and the Canary Islands.
Grows to 40 feet.

This is a beautiful specimen when allowed to develop naturally. The small white flowers are held in clusters to 10 inches. The fruit is red turning dark purple. Portugal laurel is hardier than many other laurels and will withstand sun, heat, and wind.

A number of cultivars have been developed, such as 'Myrtifolia,' with smaller leaves; and 'Variegata,' with white in the leaves.

Pseudotsuga menziesii
Douglas fir

Needled evergreen
Zones 6–9
Native to Alaska through western United States into Mexico.
Fast-growing to 200 feet tall, but usually less, and 30–60 feet wide.

The Douglas fir is unmatched as a timber tree. It produces more lumber than any other single species in the United States. It also has merit as a landscape tree. The uniform pyramid shape, when young, makes it an ideal Christmas tree.

Stiff branches droop on the lower part of this tree, but the upper branches extend upward and outward. Soft, flat, bluish-green needles are arranged spirally on the twigs. The new growth in spring is an attractive apple-green. The foliage is always fragrant and fresh smelling.

Although native to the moist Northwest where it can reach 200 feet, Douglas fir is widely adapted to soils and climate. The size varies with moisture. When grown in areas with a high water table, the roots can pancake—that is, spread close to the surface rather than grow deep down into the ground. When this happens, roots of a 60-foot tree may only be 12–18 inches deep. Many times, in new housing developments, areas are cleared leaving just a few trees around the homes. If the roots are pancaked, these trees

Prunus cerasifera

Prunus caroliniana

Prunus lusitanica

Pseudotsuga menziesii

Pryus calleryana 'Bradford'

Pyrus kawakamii

Quercus macrocarpa

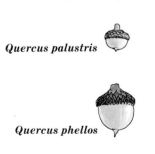

Quercus palustris

Quercus phellos

Quercus rubra

blow over in the first big wind because they no longer have the mutual support and protection of other trees.

Pyrus calleryana
Callery pear

Deciduous
Zones 5–9
Native to Eurasia, North Africa.
Moderate-growing to 25–50 feet tall and 15–20 feet wide; form varies by cultivar from broad-base oval to conical.

If any one tree illustrates what can be done through selection, it's the callery pear. The species has many good qualities: abundant early spring bloom, brilliant crimson-red fall color, shiny dark green leaves with scalloped edges, and amazing adaptability. It has three basic problems: thorns, susceptibility to fireblight, and messy, inedible fruits.

With the development of cultivars like 'Bradford,' which are thornless, fireblight resistant, and have small fruits of no inconvenience, this tree has become one of the most attractive specimens available. Add to this the difference in form between cultivars and you also have one of the most versatile specimens.

All cultivars are extremely adaptable. They stand up to pollution and other stresses of the city and can take wind, even on the coast. They are undemanding as to soil type and they are drought resistant, require little maintenance, and are relatively pest free.

All cultivars have the good qualities of the species; the difference lies in the form.

'Bradford' grows to 50 feet by 30 feet, with an oval-shape and spreading upright branches. It is thornless and usually fruitless, with spectacular fall color.

'Chanticleer' is narrower, closer to pyramidal in shape.

'Aristocrat' is pyramidal with wide-spaced, horizontal branches. It also has a glossier leaf with wavier edges.

'Faureri,' sometimes available, is a 20-foot dwarf form with an oval habit, known primarily for its profuse flower show.

Pyrus kawakamii
Evergreen pear

Evergreen
Zones 8–10
Native to Taiwan.
Moderate-growing to 30 feet; open, irregular habit.

Evergreen pear is one of the most widely used trees in California. It grows naturally into a spreading shrub but is most commonly pruned into a single or multitrunked tree. The blossoms cover the tree from late winter through spring in a showy mass of white. The leaves are a shiny light green with wavy edges. This tree is adaptable to many soil types and needs minimum care; it is easy to espalier, and good in containers near the patio or on the street.

Aphids and fireblight are two problems common to evergreen pear. Watch carefully for signs of fireblight; it can quickly destroy the tree's beauty.

Quercus species
Oaks

Oaks are among the most useful and important native trees of the United States.

Since most of the larger species are long-lived, they are preferred landscape trees where space permits. Were it not that some of them are rather difficult to transplant and require more growing space than other trees, they would be much more heavily planted.

Because oaks can reach such an impressive size and age, they are usually thought of as slow-growing trees. But this is not always true. On soil types to their liking, they are surprisingly fast-growing.

The size and shape of the acorns, and the way their "caps" are worn, are ways to tell one species of oak from another.

Oaks hybridize and, when found, such hybrids are frequently the equal of or better than their parents. Still, propagation of these superior trees continues to be a real challenge to growers.

Oak furniture and flooring are synonymous with wood that is hard and long-lasting. Park land with a high percentage of oaks is highly desirable.

Quercus acutissima
Sawtooth oak

Deciduous
Zones 7–9
Native to Korea, China, and Japan.
Moderate- to slow-growing to 30–50 feet, upcurved branching.

This oak is not very common but it has a lot of good qualities. The summer foliage is a deep, rich green that turns yellow in the fall. The gray-brown bark develops deep furrows with age.

Sawtooth oak responds well to full sun and rich, moist soil. It will grow in lesser soils.

Quercus agrifolia
Coast live oak

Evergreen
Zone 9
Native to California.
Grows 20–70 feet with a rounded, wide-spreading head.

Coast live oak has smooth gray bark, a dense head, and makes an excellent shade tree. It has shiny holly-like leaves about 1–2½ inches long.

Quercus alba
White oak

Deciduous
Zones 4–9
Native to Mexico through Texas and to Florida.
Slow-growing to 60–80 feet tall and equally wide.

White oak has a pyramidal shape when young but matures slowly to a dense and broadly rounded tree. This imposing specimen has little trouble with pests or diseases but must have well-drained, nonalkaline soil with plenty of moisture.

Quercus coccinea
Scarlet oak

Deciduous
Zones 4–9
Native to the eastern and southern United States.
Fast-growing to 50–80 feet.

Each genus of trees usually has one species that is outstanding for pronounced fall color. Among the oaks, this favored spot belongs to the scarlet oak. It thrives in full sun but does not do well in lime (basic) soils. It is also the fastest-growing oak and relatively pest-free.

Quercus macrocarpa
Bur oak

Deciduous
Zones 4–9
Native to Nova Scotia through to Texas.
Grows to 60–80 feet.

The mature oak is impressive in winter with its pillarlike trunk and its sturdy, long, and twisting branches. Younger twigs are irregularly covered with corklike ridges, sometimes extending ½-inch or so above the diameter of the twig. This hard oak is judged to withstand North Central Prairie conditions better than any other native oak species.

Quercus palustris
Pin oak

Deciduous
Zones 5–9
Native to the eastern United States.
Fairly fast-growing to 60–80 feet.

Experts generally regard the pin oak as the easiest to transplant. This fact, plus its very desirable form, glossy-fingered leaves, and rather good tolerance to a wide variety of planting sites, has made it easily the most popular native oak in the eastern United States. It is susceptible to iron chlorosis.

The drooping habit of the lower branches make this tree a poor choice where automobile or foot traffic must pass close by or underneath.

Quercus phellos
Willow oak

Deciduous
Zones 6–9
Native to New York through Florida and to Texas.
Rapid-growing to 50–80 feet; round to conical when mature.

Willow oak is the most graceful of all the oaks with slim willow-like leaves that are 1 inch wide and 2–5 inches long. This tree takes full sun or light shade and well-drained soil. In very protected areas it is partially evergreen but the bright green leaves turn yellow to rust colored in cooler climates.

Quercus agrifolia

Quercus alba

Quercus palustris

Quercus phellos

Quercus robar   *Quercus rubra*

Robinia pseudoacacia

Salix alba 'Tristis'

Quercus robur
English oak

Deciduous
Zones 5–9
Native to Africa, Europe, and Asia.
Grows to 80 feet with a wide head and a fairly short trunk.

English oak has little fall color but does not drop its leaves until late in the season. This tree is very susceptible to powdery mildew, which is not fatal but is very unsightly.

Quercus rubra
Red oak

Deciduous
Zones 5–9
Native to eastern North America
Fast-growing to 60–80 feet.

Red oak is adaptable and fast-growing with the added advantage of being fairly easy to transplant. It is second only to the scarlet oak in its fall color.

Rhamnus alaternus
Italian buckthorn

Evergreen
Zones 7–9
Native to southern Europe.
Fast-growing, tall shrub to 12–20 feet tall and equally wide.

Italian buckthorn has small, shiny green leaves and small spring flowers followed by tiny black fruits. It's valued as a high screen or hedge but responds well to shearing to any shape. This tree can be trained to be single- or multitrunked.

Rhus lancea
African sumac

Evergreen
Zones 8–10
Native to South Africa.
Slow-growing to 25 feet tall and equally wide; open spreading form.

This graceful tree has a weeping appearance due to the green and willowlike foliage. A great tree for desert heat because of its drought tolerance. African sumac is widely adapted.

Robinia pseudoacacia
Black locust

Deciduous
Zones 4–9
Native to the east central United States.
Fast-growing to 40–75 feet tall and 30–60 feet wide; often multistemmed, umbrellalike in form with sparse, open branches.

The young leaflets of black locust are silvery gray-green, turning dark green with age; yellow in fall. Fragrant, pea-shaped flowers grow in long pendant clusters and are attractive to bees. The flowers are followed by thin, flat brown pods that persists through the winter. The thorny bark is rough and deeply furrowed.

Black locust is a good choice for difficult situations. It takes heat, drought, all types of soil, and neglect. This is a quick-growing temporary tree. It is subject to several pests, most notably the locust borer. The heavy thorns, invasive and suckering root system, and weak wood make this otherwise attractive tree one to use as a last resort. After cutting it down, it may take years to eradicate suckering roots.

Salix species
Willow

Where choice is wide, willows are often frowned upon, as they have many drawbacks. The wood is brittle, it is impossible to garden around the roots, they have many pests, and they are constantly dropping leaves. However, their graceful, weeping habit is hard to match. Willows are good, quick-growing temporary trees, widely adapted to soil and climate, needing only abundant moisture.

Salix alba 'Tristis'
Golden weeping willow

Deciduous
Zones 2–9
Native to Europe, northern Africa, and Asia.
Fast-growing to 80 feet with greater spread: broad, open, round-topped, low branching.

This is one of the most beautiful varieties of weeping willow. The branches will eventually touch the ground unless the main stem is staked to 15 feet and the branches kept well pruned. The leaves are bright green to yellow-green and pale beneath.

Salix babylonica
Weeping willow

Deciduous
Zones 5–9
Native to China.
Fast-growing to 30–50 feet
with a wider spread; heavy,
round-headed, with branchlets drooping to the
ground.

Weeping willow takes its name
from its pronounced pendulous
form. The long leaves are
medium olive-green turning
yellow in the fall. The branchlets are green to brown. This
tree needs room to grow and
may need training to develop a
single trunk. It makes a good
screen and an interesting winter silhouette.

Salix matsudana
Hankow willow

Deciduous
Zones 5–9
Native to northern Asia.
Fast-growing to 35–45 feet;
pyramidal.

Two selections are more common than the species.
'Tortuosa', corkscrew willow, is a novelty grown for its
corkscrew branches and
twisted leaves. It is more of an
oddity than an effective landscape tree.
'Umbraculifera', globe willow, is a valuable plant in the
desert. Like the species, it
stands more drought than
most willows. It forms a
round-headed tree 35–40 feet
high.

Sapium sebiferum
Chinese tallow tree

Deciduous
Zones 8–9
Native to China.
Fast-growing to 35 feet tall
and equally wide; round-
headed to conical.

Chinese tallow has dense
foliage, but with an airy feeling
that provides a light shade
throughout the summer. The
leaves are aspenlike in appearance and turn bronze to bright
red after a sharp frost. Pruning
in the early stages will confine
it to a single trunk. A good
lawn or street tree, it can also
be used as a shade tree in the
patio or on the terrace. It also
makes a good screen.
This tree tolerates moist

soils but prefers acid conditions. Ample water will
encourage fast growth. The
Chinese tallow tree is a good
pest- and disease-free substitute for the poplar.

Sassafras albidum
Sassafras

Deciduous
Zones 5–9
Native to the eastern United
States.
Moderate-growing rate to
30–50 feet; irregular habit.

A tree common to eastern
hedgerows and woodlands,
sassafras seems to be all but
forgotten by nurseries selecting superior forms of other
eastern hardwoods. This is
probably due to the fact that it
is difficult to transplant. It is
best to transplant small trees
only.
Sassafras has interesting foliage and excellent yellow to red
fall color. Several shapes of the
bright green leaves may be
found on the same branch.
They vary from 2 lobes to a
1-lobe mitten shape to no lobes
at all.
The flowers on female trees
are followed by interesting
dark blue berries with bright
red stalks that are quite attractive up close.
These trees are commonly
bothered by Japanese beetles.
They are native to acid soils,
and can be effectively used in
naturalized areas, woodland
borders, parks, and other
large areas.

Schinus molle
Pepper tree

Evergreen
Zones 9–10
Native to Peru, Bolivia, and
Chile.
Fast-growing to 20–50 feet;
rounded with wide-
spreading, weeping
branches.

This pepper tree is not a
member of the true pepper
family at all, but it is a tree of
beautiful character. In its
native lands, the tree had
many uses in addition to the
welcome shade it provided.
The leaves were employed to
speed germination of seed
corn, the red berries were
ground to produce a beverage,
and the Incas apparently
further refined this drink into

Salix matsudana

Sassafras albidum

Sapium sebiferum

Sapium sebiferum

Schinus molle

Sequoiadendron
giganteum

Sequoia
sempervirens

Sophora japonica

Sorbus alnifolia

an effective intoxicant.

Schinus has a well-deserved reputation for growing rapidly with very little encouragement, accepting poor soils, scant rainfall, strong winds, and occasional frost.

The shallow root system can lift pavement and the tree is highly susceptible to aphids and black scale. Also, the fruits can become a litter problem.

Sequoia sempervirens
Coast redwood

Needled evergreen
Zones 7–10
Native to coast ranges of Oregon and California.
Although variable in height, considered a fast-growing tree to 50–70 feet in the garden; narrow pyramidal form.

Coast redwood is best adapted in the fog belt of northern California and Oregon, where it can receive year-round moisture. The attractiveness and fast-growing habit of the coast redwood has prompted plantings out of its native range throughout California.
Selected forms eliminate the problem of seedling variability.
'Aptos blue' has heavy, blue green foliage.
'Santa Cruz' is a full, dense tree with soft-textured, light green foliage.
'Los Altos' has glossy foliage, and rich green color that persists even in winter.

Sequoiadendron giganteum
Big tree, giant redwood

Needled evergreen
Zones 7–10
Native to the west slope of the Sierra Nevada mountain range from Placer County to Tulare County, occurring in disconnected groves.
Moderate-growing to as high as 350 feet in natural stands, much less in the garden; pyramidal.

There are few similarities between the big tree and the coast redwood. The big tree is more distinctly pyramidal and the foliage is denser, stiffer, and scalelike compared to the soft, airy coast redwood. Also, the giant redwood, or big tree, doesn't require constant moisture and is hardier. Foliage is

gray-green. This tree is best used in large, open areas.

Sophora japonica
Japanese pagoda tree

Deciduous
Zones 5–10
Native to Japan, Korea.
Moderate-growing to 20–30 feet, slow-growing to 50–70 feet and equally wide-spread; dense, upright form when young, becoming round and spreading with age.

The Japanese pagoda tree starts blooming when it is 8–10 years old. Then it is covered with large loose clusters of creamy-white, pea-shaped blossoms for a period lasting at least six weeks. In good cool summers it can last two months, which is quite remarkable. These trees are extremely regular in their blooming habits. They all come into bloom almost on the same day no matter where they are growing in a given geographic area—on streets, in gardens, or in parks.
The fall color of the compound leaf is a very clear yellow. This tree is ordinarily recommended for filtered shade.
Even the healthiest of Japanese pagoda trees will prune themselves. Small branches on the inside of the tree will naturally die off. In a year or so they drop and the parent branch heals over. This self-pruning process is probably due to verticillium wilt, which may develop into a significant problem. The branch die-back allows the wind to blow through these trees; consequently, they don't suffer from wind or ice-storm damage.

Sorbus alnifolia
Korean mountain ash

Deciduous
Zones 5–7
Native to Central China, Korea, and Japan.
Moderate-growing to 25–35 feet; dense oval form.

This tree has dense shiny leaves. The leaves resemble certain crabapples, and are not compound as are most of the species in this genus. The flowers are pure white, abundantly produced in small clusters like hawthorn flowers, followed by masses of bright scarlet berries in the fall. The fall foliage assumes brilliant shades of scarlet and crimson. This variety remains scarce, despite its great merits, because the seed is very difficult to germinate.

'Redbird' is even more showy than the wild species, erect-growing with fine dark green leaves; it is an abundant fruiter.

Sorbus aucuparia
European mountain ash

Deciduous
Zones 2–7
Native to Europe and Asia.
Moderate-growing to 25–30 feet; narrow, upright form rounding with maturity.

This is the most commonly grown and most popular species. Its enormous clusters of bright red berries are most showy when they color up in late summer and early fall. Its great enemies are borer insects, which are more serious the farther south it is planted. Fireblight is also a problem, making it almost impossible to grow this tree in hot, humid areas.

Having been cultivated for so long, European mountain ash has given rise to many varieties, some with yellow berries, one with doubly cut leaves, and others with distinctive habits of growth.

Stenocarpus sinuatus
Firewheel tree

Evergreen
Zones 9–10
Native to Queensland.
Moderate-growing to 15–20 feet tall and 10–15 feet wide.

This excellent subject exhibits, from the earliest, very large, beautifully designed leaves of rich glossy green. In due course, about five years, it will begin to produce the bizarre inflorescence that gives rise to the common name. Borne in fiery red clusters, the separate blooms have been likened to a miniature crown or pinwheel. The twelve or more radiating spokes are actually individual flowers so symmetrically arranged that the two- to three-inch wheel looks quite artificial. It prefers good soil on the acid side with regular

food and water, and will not suffer from partial or afternoon shade.

Stewartia koreana
Korean stewartia

Deciduous
Zones 6–9
Native to Korea.
Slow-growing to 30–35 feet; pyramidal.

The Korean stewartia is the hardiest of the various species and also has the showiest flowers. They are white with golden centers, like single camellias, and 3 inches across. Starting in early June, they open successively for a long period. The bark has an interesting mottled appearance and is a striking orange-red color in the fall. This is a lovely and unusual tree.

Stewartia pseudocamellia
Japanese stewartia

Deciduous
Zones 8–9
Native to Japan.
Slow-growing to 50–60 feet; pyramidal.

Like *Stewartia koreana*, this is an all-season performer. The bright green foliage is neat and attractive, turning shades of crimson and purple in the fall. Large white flowers with gold centers are borne in abundance over a long period in midsummer. The attractive branch silhouette and beautiful red, flaking bark are especially prominent in winter.

Styrax japonicus
Japanese snowbell, Japanese snowdrop tree

Deciduous
Zones 5–9
Native to Japan and China.
Slow- to moderate-growing to about 15–20 feet; horizontal branching forms spreading, flat-topped tree.

Observers from across the country rated this as one of the choicest small garden trees. This neat, very bushy little tree with its clean foliage and attractive zigzag habit of branching is especially nice to plant overhanging a patio, because the pendent flowers, which look like white fuchsia blossoms, are most effective when viewed from below.

They are borne in great abundance in early June so that the whole tree looks white during the long period when it is in bloom.

Japanese snowbell tolerates shade and grows best in rich, well-drained soil. It will need training to control shrubbiness but it is a good tree to garden under on the lawn or in the patio.

Syringa reticulata (S. amurensis japonica)
Japanese lilac tree

Deciduous
Zones 4–8
Native to Japan.
Moderate-growing to 20–35 feet tall and about 15–25 feet wide; open, upright, spreading branches with round outline.

This lovely and hardy little tree was popular in Victorian times, but is rarely planted today. It has many good qualities, including the large pyramidal heads of white flowers, clean, disease-free foliage, and interesting cherry-like bark. The flowers have an unusual odor similar to the fragrance of privet which is offensive to some people. They are borne in mid-June, making this the latest flowering lilac. Japanese lilac tree is very drought-resistant and will thrive where dogwoods and other less tolerant trees soon die out. It can be used as a small shade tree or as a street tree.

Tamarix aphylla
Athel tree

Deciduous
Zones 8–10
Native to the Mediterranean countries.
Fast-growing to 30–50 feet.

The athel tree is indispensable as a windbreak for the desert. It is tolerant to saline soils and commonly planted as small seedlings. Larger plants are difficult to transplant because of large tap roots. Green, jointed branches give the tree an evergreen appearance. The real leaves are very small and inconspicuous. Small pink flowers appear at the branch tips in late summer and occasionally throughout the rest of the year.

Sorbus aucuparia

Stewartia pseudocamellia

Syringa reticulata

Styrax japonicus

Taxodium distichum

Thuja occidentalis

Thuja plicata

Tilia cordata

Taxodium distichum
Bald cypress

Deciduous conifer
Zones 5–10
Native to Delaware through
 Florida and west into Texas.
Moderate- to fast-growing to
 50–100 feet.

Bald cypress is tolerant of both drought and poor drainage, and has tiny leaves that don't need raking. In fact, the leaves are too small to rake. It is deciduous and, therefore, good as a shade tree that will let in the winter sun. It has a rather slender shape that allows it to fit where space is somewhat limited.
 Few woody plants can survive in aquatic situations. The few that do, such as the bald cypress, multiply and are prominent because of their large numbers. Air is known to be important to the root systems of most plants. The bald cypress solves the problem by having the roots come up for air in the form of the cypress knees we see projecting from swamp water. In a higher setting, these knees don't form, and the cypress will thrive on dry sites.

Thuja occidentalis
American arborvitae,
northern white cedar

Needled evergreen
Zones 3–9
Native to southeastern
 Canada and the northeastern
 United States.
Slow- to moderate-growing to
 40–50 feet tall; narrow
 pyramidal

This tree displays bright green to yellow-green foliage in flat sprays on branches with up-sweeping tips. In winter, it turns an unattractive yellowish brown, except in certain selected cultivars.
 American arborvitae will tolerate wet soils, but it can topple in the wind in open, wet areas. It is more stable on drier sites. This tree makes an effective hedge or tall screen. Columnar forms, commonly sold as 'Fastigiata,' 'Columnaris,' or 'Pyramidalis,' are most useful hedge or screen trees. Other selections are available and vary in height and foliage color.

Thuja plicata
Western red cedar,
giant arborvitae, canoe
cedar

Needled evergreen
Zones 5–9
Native to Alaska through
 northern California and
 across to Montana.
Slow-growing to as high as
 130–200 feet where native,
 usually much less in
 cultivation; pyramidal.

This is an ever present tree in the northwestern United States. The foliage of the species is bright to dark green and lacy. The branches are slender.
 Western red cedar tolerates wet soils but the roots can pancake (see *Pseudotsuga menziesii*, p. 99). It takes shearing, is a valuable large hedge or screen tree, and looks great in large, open areas where lower branches can sweep the ground. This is an excellent skyline tree.
 'Fastigiata' has an upright columnar form and is an especially effective tall screen.

Tilia cordata
Littleleaf linden

Deciduous
Zones 4–9
Native to Europe.
Moderate- to fast-growing to
 60–100 feet.

This is a finely textured tree with the typical linden heart-shaped dark green leaf, only smaller (1¼–2½ inches long compared to the 3- to 5-inch leaf of most lindens). Its symmetrical habit has made it a very popular street, lawn, or shade tree, and it can even be trimmed into an effective hedge.
 The lindens can stand adverse city conditions, heat and drought, and a wide variety of soils, although they grow best in moist, fertile soils.
 In late spring or early summer, the lindens bear clusters of very fragrant yellow flowers that bring the trees alive with the buzz of bees. Flowers are followed by small papery bracts, similar to maple tree samaras.

Tsuga canadensis
Canadian eastern hemlock

Needled evergreen
Zones 4–8

Native to northeastern North America.

Moderate-growing to 60–90 feet; pyramidal.

Canadian hemlock bears graceful horizontal branches, drooping at the tips and bearing dense, flat, deep green sprays of short needles. Because of its small twigs and fine texture, it is extremely well-adapted to hard shearing and is easily trained into a thick hedge, which can be maintained at a very slowly increasing height for decades.

They thrive in deep moist loam and tolerate light shade. They resent dry winds, drought, and prolonged heat.

Young hemlocks look best in mass plantings. However, if you can wait, they do make outstanding specimens with age, especially in a lawn. Hemlock scale is a problem in New York, New Jersey, Connecticut, and Pennsylvania.

Tsuga caroliniana
Carolina hemlock

Needled evergreen
Zones 5–7
Native to the mountains of Virginia and Georgia.
Moderate-growing to 50–70 feet; pyramidal.

This fine hemlock needs a growing environment similar to the Canadian hemlock, but it is not quite as hardy. It is more tolerant of the pollution in a city environment, and it requires an acid soil. The branches are slightly pendulous, giving the Carolina hemlock a pleasing soft appearance that is less rigid and symmetrical than its Canadian counterpart.

Ulmus americana
American elm

Deciduous
Zones 3–9
Native to the eastern United States.
Fast-growing to 100 feet; vase-shaped, spreading head.

Due to the widespread attack of Dutch elm disease, the future of this tree is threatened. Dutch elm disease is caused by a fungus. The leaves of the infected trees turn yellow, then wilt and die. The sapwood, the wood directly under the bark, develops brown streaks, and eventually the entire tree dies. Researchers are actively studying the devastating Dutch elm disease in the hope of saving existing trees and providing a safe environment for new elms. Individuals or cities wishing information on preventive measures should write to either the United States Department of Agriculture, the Forest Service, or the Elm Research Institute, Harrisville, New Hampshire 03450. Sawleaf zelkova (*Zelkova serrata*, p. 108) can be used as a substitute for the American elm. It is quite similar and far less susceptible to Dutch elm disease.

Ulmus parvifolia
Chinese elm

Deciduous
Zones 5–9
Native to China and Japan.
Fast-growing to 40–60 feet; oval form.

The true Chinese elm, *Ulmus parvifolia*, is probably the most erroneously condemned tree. It is often confused with the Siberian elm, *Ulmus pumila*, which is a tree of questionable merit.

Chinese elm is a medium-sized tree that is very tolerant of alkaline, poor, and compacted soil, and of heat and drought. It has durable storm-resistant wood and small, clustered leaves that give it an open canopy. The leaves are dark green, turning pale yellow to purple in the fall. In late fall, subtle red clusters of fruit appear and add interest to the tree. The exfoliating bark, however, is this tree's best aesthetic feature. With age, the tree sheds the circular plates of its brown bark to reveal a pale yellow inner bark.

Chinese elm grows rapidly under good conditions. It is highly resistant to Dutch elm disease and the elm leaf beetle. The wood is strong, and the leaves are small and easily shredded by a rotary mower. Seedlings are variable and potential exists for the selection of superior cultivars. The current "elm phobia," due to Dutch elm disease, should be ignored in the case of this fine tree.

Tsuga canadensis

Ulmus americana

Ulmus parvifolia

Zelkova serrata

Ziziphus jujuba

Vitex agnus-castus
Chaste tree, hemp tree

Evergreen
Zones 9–10
Native to southern Europe.
Slow-growing in cold climates
 and faster-growing in warm
 climates to 6–20 feet; broad
 and spreading.

Chaste tree is often multitrunked. The leaflets are dark
green above and gray beneath.
This tree flowers best with
summer heat; showy lilac-blue
flowers bloom in late summer
and early fall. The tree is best
grown in full sun. In hot climates, it makes a good shade
tree when trained high.

Vitex lucens
*New Zealand chaste tree,
 puriri*

Evergreen
Zones 9–10
Native to New Zealand.
Slow- to moderate-growing to
 40–60 feet; round, spreading.

The foliage of the New Zealand
chaste tree is particularly
handsome with large rich
green compound leaves of five
ruffled 3-inch leaflets. The
small, pink, bell-shaped
flowers are followed by rose-
red, cherrylike, inedible fruits.
The New Zealand chaste tree
requires rich soil that is high in
organic soil content.

Zelkova serrata
*Sawleaf zelkova, Japanese
zelkova*

Deciduous
Zones 5–9

Native to Japan and Korea.
Moderate- to fast-growing to
 50–60 feet tall and equally as
 wide; round-headed,
 eventually vase-shaped.

Japanese zelkova has been
heavily pushed as a substitute
for its close relative, the
American elm. The foliage is
similar to the elms; it turns
shades of yellow or red in fall,
the most common color being
russet. With age, the gray
bark takes on an attractive
mottling.
 This tree is not immune to
Dutch elm disease, but it has a
far better chance of surviving
than the American elm. Wilt is
also a problem on sawleaf
zelkova.

Ziziphus jujuba
Chinese jujube

Deciduous
Zones 6–9
Native to southeastern
 Europe and China.
Grows to 15–25 feet;
 vase-shaped.

Chinese jujube is a widely
adapted dual-purpose tree. It
is especially valuable in the
high and low desert, being able
to stand alkaline or saline soils
and drought. Small, glossy
green leaves are markedly
veined. Small, yellow flowers
are followed by a fall crop of
fruits with the taste of a meaty
apple. When dried and can-
died, they taste like dates.
The gnarled, rather rough
trunk and drooping thorned
branches are picturesque in
winter.

Vitex agnus-castus

Index

Common names of trees are listed and cross-referenced to the botanical names. Numbers in bold indicate the principal description; numbers in italics indicate an illustration.

Front cover: *Magnolia soulangiana*, the saucer magnolia, blooms in early spring before the leaves appear. See page 87.

Back cover: The maple is one of the best trees for fall color. Various maples (*Acer* species) are listed on pages 61–63.

Title page: An elm tree (*Ulmus* species) softens the landscape around an isolated farm in Ohio. Elms are described on page 107.

U.S. MEASURE AND METRIC MEASURE CONVERSION CHART

	Symbol	**Formulas for exact measure**			**Rounded measures for quick reference**				
		When you know:	Multiply by:	To find:					
Mass (weight)	oz	ounces	28.35	grams	1 oz	=	2 tbsp	=	30 g
	lb	pounds	0.45	kilograms	4 oz	=	½ c	=	115 g
	g	grams	0.035	ounces	8 oz	=	1 c	=	225 g
	kg	kilograms	2.2	pounds	16 oz	=	1 lb	=	450 g
					32 oz	=	2 lb	=	900 g
					36 oz	=	2¼ lb	=	1000 g (1 kg)
Volume	tsp	teaspoons	5	milliliters	¼ tsp	=	1/24 oz	=	1 ml
	tbsp	tablespoons	15	milliliters	½ tsp	=	1/12 oz	=	2 ml
	fl oz	fluid ounces	29.57	milliliters	1 tsp	=	1/6 oz	=	5 ml
	c	cups	0.24	liters	1 tbsp	=	½ oz	=	15 ml
	pt	pints	0.47	liters	1 c	=	8 oz	=	250 ml
	qt	quarts	0.95	liters	2 c (1 pt)	=	16 oz	=	500 ml
	gal	gallons	3.785	liters	4 c (1 qt)	=	32 oz	=	1 l
	ml	milliliters	0.034	fluid ounces	4 qt (1 gal)	=	128 oz	=	3¾ l
Length	in.	inches	2.54	centimeters	⅜ in.	=			1 cm
	ft	feet	30.48	centimeters	1 in.	=			2.5 cm
	yd	yards	0.9144	meters	2 in.	=			5 cm
	mi	miles	1.609	kilometers	2½ in.	=			6.5 cm
	km	kilometers	.621	miles	12 in. (1 ft)	=			30 cm
	m	meters	1.094	yards	1 yd	=			90 cm
	cm	centimeters	0.39	inches	100 ft	=			30 m
					1 mi	=			1.6 km
Temperature	F°	Fahrenheit	5/9 (after subtracting 32)	Celsius	32° F	=			0° C
					68° F	=			20° C
	C°	Celsius	9/5 +32	Fahrenheit	212° F	=			100° C
Area	in.²	square inches	6.452	square centimeters	1 in.²	=			6.5 cm²
					1 ft²	=			930 cm²
	ft²	square feet	929	square centimeters	1 yd²	=			8360 cm²
					1 a	=			4050 cm²
	yd²	square yards	8361	square centimeters					
	a	acres	4047	(hectares) square meters					